THE VICTIM OF PREJUDICE

The Victim of Prejudice

By Mary Hays

edited and with an introduction by Eleanor Ty

broadview literary texts

Canadian Cataloguing in Publication Data

Hays, Mary, 1759/60-1843
    The victim of prejudice

(Broadview Literary Texts)
ISBN 0-921149-37-9

I. Ty, Eleanor Rose, 1958- . II. Title. III. Series.

PR4769.H6V5   1994   823'.7   C92-093421-8

Broadview Press
Post Office Box 1243, Peterborough, Ontario, Canada K9J 7H5

in the United States of America:
3576 California Road, Orchard Park, NY 14127

in the United Kingdom:
B.R.A.D. Book Representation & Distribution Ltd.,
244A, London Road, Hadleigh, Essex. SS7 2DE

Broadview Press gratefully acknowledges the support of the Canada
Council, the Ontario Arts Council, and the Ministry of Canadian Heritage.

PRINTED IN CANADA

Contents

Editor's Introduction

BY 1799, THE YEAR *The Victim of Prejudice* was published, Mary Hays was almost forty years old and had already lived the more radical and exciting half of her life.[1] Her first novel, *Memoirs of Emma Courtney*, published in −1796, made her something of a notorious celebrity in the literary circles of London. The book was based on her love and pursuit of the Cambridge mathematician and reformer, William Frend. Frend advocated parliamentary reform, and in 1793 was tried and discharged by Cambridge University for his pamphlet "Peace and Union," which criticized the government and religion and contained a diatribe against war. He moved to London a year later and became involved with Jacobins and Dissenters such as George Dyer, Thomas Holcroft, William Godwin, and Mary Hays. From the time of their meeting he carried on a correspondence with Hays, but evidently did not reciprocate her feelings for him. The disappointed Hays turned to Godwin for consolation and advice. On his recommendation, she gathered together her letters to both men, and used them in her philosophical novel which attempted to explore the link between reason and a woman's passion.

Emma Courtney's unorthodox heroine and its daring subject matter did not prevent it from receiving warm praise from critics when it first appeared. The *Analytical Review* and the *Monthly Magazine* both gave it positive reviews and commended its good sense and its potential for instruction.[2] The more conservative publications, the *Critical Review* and the *British Critic,* were hesitant about the revolutionary and political implications of the outspoken and impassioned female character.[3] On the whole, the book was fairly successful.

A few years later, however, the novel and its author became the target of much abuse and satire. This hostility was due, in part, to the strong anti-Jacobin sentiment which rose steadily as the decade progressed. A more direct cause was the publication of William Godwin's *Memoirs of the Author of a Vindication of the Rights of Woman* (1798)[4] with the account of Wollstonecraft's youthful infatuation for the married Henry Fuseli, her affair with American Gilbert Imlay, her two suicide attempts, and her illegitimate child. Following these revelations, moralists were quick to equate those who spoke for women's rights with sexual liberty and licentiousness. After Wollstonecraft's death, Hays, as her disciple, bore the brunt of much of the vehemence of the conservative side of the "war of ideas."[5] Along with Anna Laetitia Barbauld, Mary Robinson, Charlotte Smith, Helen Maria Williams, and others, Hays was cited among Wollstonecraft's female band of rebels who despise "Nature's law" in the Reverend Richard Polwhele's poem *The Unsex'd Females* (1798). Hays was also caricatured in a couple of novels published at this time. In Charles Lloyd's *Edmund Oliver* (1798), which satirizes Coleridge and the English Jacobins, Hays appears as Lady Gertrude Sinclair. Hays' scathing letter condemning Elizabeth Hamilton's *Letters of a Hindoo Raja* (1796) might have prompted Hamilton to model the comic female philosopher Bridgetina Botherim after Hays in *Memoirs of Modern Philosophers* (1800).[6] As a result, Hays is now remembered more as an object of ridicule than as a serious feminist thinker.

Hays was certainly not the first to argue for the need to re-examine the social and cultural construction of gender. Mary Astell, Catherine Macaulay, and Mary Wollstonecraft all perceived that gender difference was not simply the result of essential biological distinctions, but that, to a far greater extent, it was due to the way female subjectivity was constituted in the seventeenth and eighteenth centuries. While they diverged in their opinions about the proper sphere for females, they all shared the belief that education was the key to improving women's mental capabilities and to ameliorating their social and economic condition.[7] Hays' most articulate essays on the subject were published in the 1790s. Like Thomas Paine, William Godwin, Mary Wollstonecraft, Thomas Holcroft, Elizabeth Inchbald, and William Blake, among others, Hays saw the French Revolution of 1789 as the dawning of a new age of liberalism and egalitarianism. Her works written during this time were infused with a sense of enthusiasm for social and political change in both the private and public spheres.

Hays' radicalism involved what feminists today would call the politics of the personal. At age seventeen, she fell in love with fellow Dissenter John Eccles, who acted as her teacher as well as her lover. Initially, both Hays' recently widowed mother and Eccles' family disapproved of the relationship. For two years the couple carried on a secret correspondence until the families finally approved of their engagement in 1780. Tragically, however, the long-awaited consummation of their romance never occurred because Eccles died from fever just before their marriage. In a note to her album of letters Hays called the day of his death the "fatal day, which blasted all the fond hopes of my youth."[8] Thus, barely out of adolescence, she felt deprived of the culturally sanctioned subject position of wife and mother. Denied marriage and its subsequent social and economic security, Hays had to create her own identity as a female radical thinker. In effect, the works that deal specifically with the subject of woman's position in society can be read not only as political tracts, but also as efforts to authenticate her own subjectivity in an intellectual climate dominated largely by males.

Two of the most pervasive themes of her works published in the 1790s are woman's economic dependence and female sexual identity, subjects Mary Wollstonecraft also examines in her polemical unfinished novel, *The Wrongs of Woman, or Maria* (1798). Hays' earliest effort on gender issues, *Letters and Essays, Moral and Miscellaneous* (1793), which contains two short stories by her sister Eliza, attempts to find ways to make women more useful in society and calls for a "reformation of manners."[9] Like Wollstonecraft in *A Vindication of the Rights of Woman* (1792), Hays employs a combination of rational and sentimental discourses, the essay, and the anecdote, to argue for the recognition of woman's moral and intellectual worth:

> It is time for degraded woman to assert her right to reason. . . . The frivolity and voluptuousness, in which they have hitherto been educated, have had a large share in the general corruption of manners; this frivolity the sensible vindicator of our rights justly attributes to the entire dependence in which we are trained. Young women without fortunes, if they do not chance to marry. . . have scarce any other resources than in servitude, or prostitution. I never see, without indignation, those trades, which ought to be appropriated only

to women, almost entirely engrossed by men, hab-
erdashery, millinery, & even mantua-making.
(Garland, 84–5)

This passage, intense and forthright, is characteristic
of her prose writing. She often begins with a general
observation, cites a few specific examples or illustrations,
and ends with her opinion on how to correct the problem.
They are for the most part practical, rather than idealistic
solutions. At times, she calls upon reason and the interest
of humanity for support; at others, she uses religious and
scriptural authorities. When she came to write her first
novel, she thematized many of the issues raised in *Letters
and Essays*, dramatizing the effects of eighteenth-century
social and cultural prejudices through the adventures of
her heroine, Emma Courtney.

At once energetic and oppressive, *Memoirs of Emma
Courtney* presents a much more powerful case for her arguments in its portrayal of female imprisonment. Struc-
turally as well as thematically, Hays demonstrates her contention that women are prevented from participating in
many of the important functions of society, or to use one
of her metaphors, they are "confined within a magic circle."[10] Written partly in an epistolary form, partly as
memoirs, *Emma Courtney* traps both the reader of the
novel and the reader within the text, young Augustus, in
an endless circle of suffocating repetition. The heroine's
sexual and intellectual disappointments are mirrored by
the novel's incessant, stifling pattern of frustrated desire
and unfulfilled expectations in a style that is deliberately
one-sided. Through a strong first-person narration, we
hear Emma's story of exclusion, of rejection, and of self-
torture. Hardly anyone else's voice is heard so that the
reader's attention is focused on her affecting plight.

What Hays believes to be the female experience of confinement by the "constitutions of society"[11] becomes literal in the novel as we, too, experience narrative entrapment.

Another important achievement of the novel is that Hays' heroine, Emma Courtney, like Wollstonecraft's Maria in *The Wrongs of Woman*, dares to assert female sexuality and desire. The notion that women had or could express sexual feelings was one that eighteenth-century moralists and authors of conduct books tried hard to deny or ignore. Emma pronounces: "I feel that I am neither a philosopher, nor a heroine—but a *woman, to whom education has given a sexual character.*"[12] In other words, as twentieth-century theorist Julia Kristeva suggests, "the knowing subject is also a *desiring* subject, and the paths of desire ensnarl the paths of knowledge."[13] In contrast to Hays' position is that of conservative novelist Jane West, whose novel *A Gossip's Story* (1796) Hays reviewed in the January 1797 issue of the *Analytical Review*. West portrays the ideal wife as a self-effacing subject. In her novel, the father tells his daughter that she must place her husband's needs before hers at all times:

> There is no part of the female character dearer to us men, than the idea that you are the soothers of our inquietudes, the solacers of our sorrow, the sympathizing friends to whom we may at all times retire for comfort, in every distress.[14]

In fact, *jouissance*, the pleasures of the physical and material world, have no legitimate place in West's conception of the ideal marital relationship. The father advises his daughter: "Exert the powers of your understanding, my dear child. . . . You are commanded to prepare yourself for a spiritual world, not to languish out life in luxurious softness."[15] This position of submission and resignation is one which both Hays and Wollstonecraft reject in their prose and their fiction.

After the publication of her first novel, Hays contributed short articles on topics ranging from women's education to gender differentiation and political philosophy to the *Monthly Magazine*. Many of these letters were signed M.H. She also reviewed novels for the *Analytical Review*, whose fiction editor in 1796 to early 1797 was Mary Wollstonecraft.[16] (Hays wrote an unsigned obituary of Wollstonecraft in the *Monthly Magazine* of September 1797.) *Appeal to the Men of Great Britain in Behalf of Women* (1798) was published anonymously and has been attributed subsequently to Hays. The *Appeal* stresses the necessity of reforming the system of education for women and refutes the claim that women are naturally inferior to men. Its style is spirited and direct, in contrast to anecdotal and illustrative approach of *Letters and Essays*. In this work too, Hays attempts to point out that the character of women is socially and culturally constructed, rather than inherently weak and lacking in abilities:

> Of all the systems. . . which human nature in its moments of intoxication has produced; that which men have contrived with a view to forming the minds, and regulating the conduct of women, is perhaps the most completely absurd.[17]

Katharine Rogers suggests that compared to Wollstonecraft's *Rights of Woman*, Hays' *Appeal* is less theoretical and more pragmatic: "Hays's basic strategy. . . is to confront conventional formulas with daily experience, so as to demonstrate by common sense their internal inconsistencies and their deviations from what actually happens and what is obviously desirable."[18] This ability to particularize and render concrete her feminist assertions is perhaps what makes her fiction so moving and powerful.

***

Hays' final explicitly feminist work published in the decade of the 1790s was *The Victim of Prejudice* (1799). Like her first novel, *Emma Courtney*, *Victim* deliberately incorporates the arguments she made in her prose writings and illustrates them through a dramatic — and sometimes melodramatic — narrative. The form of fictional autobiography enables Hays once again to make use of a strong female voice to authenticate woman's experience. And also like *Emma Courtney*, *Victim* is concerned with female economic and social dependence, sexuality, and subjectivity. But Hays adds another important dimension to this novel: the critique of social hierarchy based on class. Gary Kelly says that the work has a "politically suggestive title" and describes it as

> another English Jacobin novel. . . like Godwin's *Things as They Are* and Wollstonecraft's *Wrongs of Woman*. . . . It attacks the denaturing effects of property and rank on individual identity and domestic affections, uses a Gothic plot of flight and pursuit to dramatize oppression, deploys Gothic settings of prisons and tribunals to represent the operation of ideology as *force majeure*, dramatizes social conflict through 'philosophical' dialogue, and broadens the social critique by inset or parallel narratives.[19]

Though it appeared only three years after the publication of her first novel, *Victim* is markedly different. Hays was much less hopeful about the changes that the example of the French Revolution would bring about in England, and as a result, this novel is less idealistic and more sombre in tone. Like Wollstonecraft's *Wrongs of Woman* in spirit and intent, *Victim* is a catalogue of possible "wrongs" or acts of social injustice perpetrated on the eighteenth-century middle-class female.

Hays sets out to dispel Edmund Burke's myth of the benevolent patriarch as the adequate head or monarch of the residents of his estates. In *Reflections on the Revolution in France* (1790) and in *A Letter to a Member of the National Assembly* (1791), Burke argued that only the sanctity of the domestic family would preserve England from the forces of anarchy, the destruction of society, and the loss of national heritage. As Claudia Johnson points out:

> [Burke] describes what happens when a political system and the dominant figures within it no longer command the sentimental life—the aspirations, inhibitions, and loyalties—of its subjects. In self-proclaimed contrast to crazed French ideologues who would break with time-honored traditions in order to create a new society based on rational principles, Burke apotheosizes the patriarchal ideal and the social and sentimental structures which enforce it: the retired life of the country gentleman, the orderly transmission of property, the stabilizing principle of generational continuity, the grateful deference of youth to venerable age, and of course the chastity of wives and daughters which alone can guarantee the social identity of men and heirs.[20]

What Hays and other female radical thinkers of the 1790s saw as problematic in Burke's theories was the idealization of the male figure of authority. In novels such as *Victim of Prejudice, Wrongs of Woman, Desmond, A Simple Story*, and others written in the late eighteenth century, Hays, Wollstonecraft, Charlotte Smith, and Elizabeth Inchbald, among others, all question this notion of the benevolent patriarch by showing how fathers and husbands could become despotic and abusive, and therefore unfit to govern their families, or little "monarchies."[21]

A statement made by Hays almost twenty years after the publication of *Reflections on the Revolution in France* shows the extent of the influence on her of Burke's ideas and the revolutionary spirit of the times. As Gary Kelly notes, in writing about Queen Caroline in her *Memoirs of Queens, Illustrious and Celebrated* (1821), "Hays deliberately recalls the place of woman in the Revolution debate inaugurated by Burke at the beginning of the 1790s."[22] Hays writes:

> Burke, had he now lived, would have retraced his assertion, that the age of chivalry had passed away; it revived, in all its impassioned fervour, amidst the soberest and gravest people in the civilized world. Every manly mind shrank from the idea of driving, by protracted and endless persecutions, a desolate unprotected female from her family, her rank, from society and from the world. *Woman* considered it as a common cause against the despotism and tyranny of man.[23]

The link between woman and rebellion or woman as an emblem of resistance to male authority is certainly one of the dominant figures in her second novel. Written at the end of the revolutionary decade, *Victim of Prejudice* exploits the politicized climate and demonstrates the uneasy tensions and potentially explosive situations between those with power and those without, between male and female, between oppressor and victim.

The hero, or more accurately, the anti hero, Sir Peter Osborne, is the complete opposite of the Burkean ideal and is devoid of any sense of kindness or generosity towards his tenants. As the representative patriarch, he should protect rather than take advantage of those under his authority. Hays shows the possible abuses of those with rank and economic power by making Osborne the Gothic-like villain who indefatigably pursues the heroine, Mary Raymond. Unlike novels like Ann Radcliffe's *The Mysteries of Udolpho* (1794), the dark villain is not paired with an opposite figure—a young, worthy suitor who rescues the heroine at the end. In fact in the world of the *Victim of Prejudice*, there is no hero. Symbolically, it is Osborne who expels Mary from an Eden-like existence with the Nevilles and forces her to go to the complex, sinister world of the city where she loses her "innocence" both physically and intellectually. At their first encounter, he catches Mary stealing a cluster of grapes from his greenhouse and calls her "a true daughter of Eve" (14) because of her innocence, beauty, and transgression. This name soon becomes even more appropriate: shortly after the attempted theft of the forbidden fruit, Mary loses her near-paradisal childhood existence with her benevolent guardian in Monmouthshire.

Another irony of this appellation is that it links the then virginal Mary with the temptress figure of Eve. It is perhaps not coincidental that two of the most prominent women of the Bible are fused in the character of Mary. In Osborne's limited understanding, all women are stereotyped as either the mother or the whore, the angel or the mistress. Mary unwittingly becomes the object of Osborne's desire, and never gets a chance to articulate her wishes or speak as a subject. He sees her only as his "other," projecting his desire onto her and refusing to treat her as the individual that she is. His stereotypical and automatic categorization of her is a form of victimization. This is literalized through his manipulations; she is later reduced to a "daughter of Eve," a figure of temptation in the eyes of men.

Aside from being the object of desire, Mary also represents the oppressed and the defenceless. In her next encounter with Osborne, she receives lashes from his whip while trying to shelter a hare from him. Mary is linked lexically to the little animal: she describes it here as a "panting victim" (21) while she later depicts herself as a "helpless, devoted victim," "panting, half-breathless with emotion" (135). Implicitly, Hays suggests that the aristocratic Osborne desires to sport with her much in the same way as he does with the hare, chasing it and eventually killing it in the guise of adventure. Rather than embodying the Burkean ideal of the benevolent patriarch, Sir Peter abuses his privileges of power and peerage, giving in to his lascivious needs, to his "sport," rather than considering the good of the community of which Mary is part.

Earlier, in her *Appeal to the Men of Great Britain*, Hays had already expressed her reservations about giving power to men merely on the basis of their gender: "As matters now stand, it is very difficult to decide, where authority should in prudence begin, or where it ought in justice to end" (287). Protesting against "things as they are," she asks: "in forming the laws by which women are governed, . . . have not men. . . consulted more their own conveniency, comfort, and dignity, as far as their judgement and foresight served them than that of women?" (158–9). In *Victim of Prejudice* she demonstrates how "having no hand in forming [the laws]," women become the "sufferers" (*Appeal*, 159). Mary is not the only "victim" in the novel: she seems destined to repeat or replicate the sensational and melodramatic life of her mother. At one time admired and loved by Mr. Raymond, the Mary of the first generation was also a "victim of the injustice, of the prejudices of society" (66). Like her daughter, the mother blames society for her destruction:

> *Law* completes the triumph of injustice. The despotism of man rendered me weak, his vices betrayed me into shame, a barbarous policy stifled returning dignity, prejudice robbed me of the means of independence. . . (68)

In the eyes of the world, the degrading circumstances surrounding Mary's birth are enough to exclude her from respectable society. Hays is critical of a society which ranks people mainly according to their class and economic circumstances. The young heroine's education and accomplishments, her dignity and character, signify nothing in such a culture. She laments: "While the practice of the world opposes the principles of the sage, education is a fallacious effort, morals an empty theory, and sentiment a delusive dream" (33).

Despite her determination not to fall prey to seduction like her mother, the second Mary ends up with an equally tragic fate. Her worst nightmares become real in the novel, giving the work a dreamlike, Gothic quality. As she peruses her mother's memoirs, Mary becomes the reader within the narrative, whose reactions to the tale help to define our own. She is unable to transcend the confining web of the story, and becomes enmeshed by the words. She feels "a sense of oppression, almost to suffocation" and goes out into the "dark and stormy" night in order to relieve herself of her anguish (71). Trying to wash away her pain, she stays out in the howling wind and rain, but finds herself unable to escape the narrative:

> I recalled to my remembrance the image of my wretched mother: I beheld her, in idea, abandoned to infamy, cast out of society, stained with blood, expiring on a scaffold, unpitied and unwept. I clasped my hands in agony; terrors assailed me till then unknown; the blood froze in my veins; a shuddering horror crept through my heart. . . (72)

Because Mary was abandoned as an infant, the image that she sees here of her mother is an imagined rather than a recollected one. The terror that she experiences is not only for her mother's experiences in the past, but also for herself, as she feels the danger of reliving her mother's life.

Replication and literalization[24] are made more explicit in yet another instance. After her rape, Mary sees her "wretched mother" in "visionary form" (123):

> One moment, methought I beheld her in the arms of her seducer, revelling in licentious pleasure; the next, I saw her haggard, intoxicated, self-abandoned, joining in the midnight riot; and, in an instant, . . . covered with blood, accused of murder, shrieking in horrible despair . . . . Then, all pallid and ghastly, with clasped hands, . . . and agonizing earnestness, she seemed to urge me to take example from her fate! (123)

The ghostly nightmare ends with Mary clasping her parent "in a last embrace" (123). It is as if Mary subconsciously desires to be linked with her mother and her disgrace. This evocation of the past seems to be a physical and mental manifestation of the desire to return to the marginalised maternal.[25] Hays demonstrates the ambivalence a woman feels for what Lacan has called a world dominated by the Law of the Father.[26] The emphasis of maternal figures in dreams and nightmares, of the disruptive, may suggest a move in the direction of what contemporary psychoanalytic feminist theory terms the pre-Oedipal mother-child relation, even if this move frequently entails danger, death, or exclusion from the symbolic order.[27]

This mother-daughter link and the subsequent literal re-enactment[28] of the first Mary's written memoirs create much of the tension and the sense of foreboding in the novel. As Mary imagines her mother "abandoned to infamy, cast out of society, stained with blood, . . . unpitied and unwept" (72), she is also prescribing and envisioning her own future. Except for the murder of her seducer, Mary's life follows her mother's: she is systematically seduced, abandoned, and cast out of society. That Hays understood the consequences that arise from a return to the maternal is revealed when she associates it with betrayal and exclusion from the male symbolic order. Attractive as the mother-daughter connection may be, its cost is undeniably high. The attempts of both Marys to oppose and curtail masculine desire only create further constraints in their lives. Yearning for more space and freedom, they become physically and spiritually more constricted. In her depiction of the failure of the maternal, Hays recognizes that the refusal to yield to the Father's Law brings about marginalisation and isolation under the specific historical and social circumstances in which she and her heroines live.

Furthermore, the seduction and abandonment of Mary Raymond is not only a transcription of events that transpire within this novel, but also a replication – or what Margaret Homans would call a "literalization" – of a more figurative earlier text. The device of the kidnapped heroine was common enough by the 1790s,[29] but Hays was very likely thinking back to the mid-century novel *Clarissa*, by Samuel Richardson. There is evidence to suggest that Hays was rewriting *Clarissa* from a feminist perspective. Earlier, in an essay "On Novel Writing" published in the *Monthly Magazine* of September 1797, she had expressed her disagreement with Samuel Johnson, who believed that fictional narratives should exhibit "perfect models of virtue."[30] She criticizes Richardson's *Clarissa* as an example of a character who is depicted too perfectly:

> the character of Clarissa, a beautiful superstructure upon a false and airy foundation, can never be regarded as a model for imitation. It is the portrait of an ideal being, placed in circumstances equally ideal, far removed from common life and human feelings.[31]

According to Hays, Richardson's novel violates principles of "truth and nature" and abounds with "absurd superstitions and ludicrous prejudices" (180). Preferring the "real" to the ideal, Hays questions: "why should we seek to deceive . . . by illusive representations of life? Why should we not rather paint [life] as it really exists, mingled with imperfection, and discoloured by passion?" (180).

Hays' rejection of "illusive" or figurative representations can be explained in Homans' terms as a manifestation of a woman writer's lingering attachment to the pre-Oedipal, literal language as opposed to a son's whole-hearted embrace of the symbolic, figurative one associated with the Father. In the depiction of women in literature, figurative or ideal representations often entail the death or destruction of the real.[32] That Hays was aware of, and uncomfortable with, this notion is revealed in her opposition to iconic representations of good and evil. Arguing that such delineations are not "consistent with truth and fact," she writes: "Human nature seems to be at an equal distance from the humiliating descriptions of certain ascetic moralists, and the exaggerated eulogiums of enthusiasts. Gradations, almost imperceptible, of light and shade, must mingle in every true portrait of the human mind" (180). Hence, in *Victim of Prejudice* the heroine is neither the virgin Mary, despite her name, nor the temptress Eve, as Sir Osborne believes. She is not "wholly or disinterestedly virtuous or vicious" (180) but a complex and probable human being.

That Hays intended her readers to think of *Clarissa* as an intertext to her own novel is confirmed by the many similarities between the two works. Like Clarissa, Mary is from an untitled middle-class family and is courted by an aristocrat. Both heroines are transported from their homes by deceit to the London residences of the villain and rakes. Both are raped and dishonoured by their abductors, and live long enough to exclaim against their fate in writing, Clarissa in her numerous epistles and Mary in her memoirs.

However, even more significant are the differences between the two texts. Hays reworks Richardson's material according to her beliefs: her heroine is not a paragon, nor is she placed in ideal circumstances. Changing the *dénouement*, Hays does not end her novel with the trium-

phant death of the heroine, but instead uses tragic events
to illustrate the injustice of late eighteenth-century social
customs and laws, and the abuse of patriarchal authority.
There is a degree of difference in the way Richardson and
Hays handle the realistic, brutal consequences of the rape.
Richardson's Clarissa does not endure the mockery, jeers,
and condemnation of servants, friends, tradesmen, and
prospective employers in the same way that Hays' Mary
does. To a certain extent, Richardson shifts the focus to
a more ethereal, spiritual realm; Hays dwells on the sordid
details of her heroine's poverty, unemployment, and even
starvation after the sexual defilement. Unlike Clarissa,
Mary does not transcend the physical and the corporeal
to become a symbolic representation of Christian fortitude or female virtue; instead, she remains rooted in the
social and the real.

Following the rape, Hays uses a stock character of
sentimental fiction, that of the suffering heroine, or virtue
in distress, to illustrate her views on gender and class in-
equality. Mary's plight reveals how the existing justice
system fails to protect, and in fact, aids in oppressing the
wronged in society. Because of her mother's reputation
as a whore and a murderer, her insufficient knowledge of
the city, and her lack of social connections, Mary finds it
difficult to convince anyone that she was brutally violated.
She threatens Osborne with legal proceedings, but he
jeers at her: "Who will credit the tale you mean to tell?
. . . Who would support you against my wealth and influence? How would your delicacy shrink from the idea of
becoming, in open court, the sport of ribaldry, the theme
of obscene jesters?" (119). As Hays suggests in her ad-
vertisement, because of the "too-great stress laid on the
reputation for chastity in woman," Mary has difficulty in
retaining her dignity and self-respect. Paraphrasing God-

win's philosophy, she demands "liberty," and proclaims: "when the mind is determined," one cannot "fetter the body" by "feeble restraints" (118). However, her worthy resolutions soon fail: she cannot battle hunger, cold, and poverty with her philosophic ideals. In her struggle to be independent, Mary can overcome neither eighteenth-century gender and class prejudices, nor the value system of a materialistic and morally corrupt society. Eventually she succumbs to despair, unable to conceive of herself as something other than a victim or the tragic heroine of sentimental fiction.

While we may be bothered by Mary's stubbornness and her insistence on her freedom at all costs, we cannot help but sympathize with her lack of choice as she desperately clings to the only thing left intact: her self-esteem. Preferring "disgrace, indigence, contempt" to "the censure of [her] own heart" (129), Mary tries to find work as a companion, attempts to teach drawing, aspires to learn engraving, embroidery, even copying, but is rejected in all trades because she is a woman with a tarnished reputation. All the men she encounters view her only as a sexual being, not a serious worker. She complains:

> I sought only the base means of subsistence: amidst the luxuriant and the opulent . . . . I put in no claims either for happiness, for gratification . . . yet, surely, I had a right to exist!—For what crime was I driven from society? I seemed to myself like an animal entangled in the toils of the hunter. (141)

This passage is important because it raises a number of issues familiar to readers of Hays' work. First, it links the theme of economic dependence with that of the outcast or victim. In the bourgeois economy of late eighteenth-century England, financial independence was one way of becoming acceptable to society. Single women who had few chances of becoming financially secure were exiles in the system. Second, the fact that Mary is willing to work in male-dominated trades such as engraving, but is denied the opportunity, shows Hays' awareness of the social and cultural construction of gender difference. Hays demonstrates through Mary that women become marginalised not because of what they are, but because of what society expects them to do and to be.

Finally, Hays links women here with animals, traditionally regarded as lower than humans in rank on the scale of beings. Mary compares herself to an "animal entangled in the toils of the hunter," implicitly associating the attitude of the men in the community with Osborne, who had earlier tried to "sport" with her as he did with a hare. Customs and institutions make woman into a primitive "Other" or lower creature who then has to struggle to survive with only the "base means of existence" in society. Deprived of economic power and unable to use her intellectual capabilities, she is reduced to a subjectivity based on the instinctive and sensual, qualities both Hays and Wollstonecraft deplored in women. Hays' use of animal and hunting imagery to describe women is similar to that of Wollstonecraft in her novel written around the same period. In *The Wrongs of Woman*, Jemima, the servant turned prison warden, complains that she was "hunted from family to family," and "had not even the chance of being considered as a fellow-creature . . . . Fate dragged [her] through the very kennels of society."[33] Wollstonecraft's heroine, Maria, also describes herself as an animal as she flees from her husband: "I was hunted like an infected beast, from three different apartments"

(178). These metaphors reveal the sense of helplessness and degradation which result from both authors' experiences as women in eighteenth century male dominated so ciety.

Ironically, what the heroine of Hays' second novel is attempting to escape from is what her first heroine wishes to be. After the rape, Mary Raymond longs to be free of her sexuality, while Emma Courtney only wants her sexuality to be recognized. This reversal of ideas is not so much a contradiction in Hays' thinking as it is a reflection of her attempt to grapple with the vexed question of woman's desire. Hays yearns for the recognition of female sexuality, but on woman's terms. Her heroines do not want to be merely the object of man's desire, but rather a desiring subject whose intellectual, social, and psychological life remains and is not threatened. Mary Raymond is not without desire; she loved William Pelham at one point. But the kind of relationship offered to her by Osborne is inadequate, as it is strictly on his terms, and is dependent upon desires which Luce Irigaray would call "specularized."[34]

The problem of female sexuality turned into a personal one for Hays sometime in the spring of 1799, shortly after the publication of her second novel. At this time she and Charles Lloyd were friends and corresponded with each other. According to Robert Southey, Hays was depressed and exhausted one evening, and cried in front of Lloyd. He was sympathetic to her, but afterwards told his friends that she was in love with him, offered herself to him that night, was rejected, and broke into tears. When confronted with the truth, Lloyd excused his falsehoods by referring to her friendships with Godwin and William Frend, and to the events in her novel, *Emma Courtney*. Though he apologized to her, his version of the incident left its mark. Coleridge, Thomas Manning, and Charles Lamb talked about "Lloyd's amours with Mary Hays,"[35] the latter with more sympathy than the former two. In a letter composed on February 8, 1800, Charles Lamb wrote that Lloyd's treatment of Hays was "shockingly & nauseously indelicate."[36] Despite her spirit and intelligence, the false rumour brought Hays down to the level of the sensual and sexual, much like her heroine. Her attempts to theorize on female sexuality and desire were not seen at the intellectual and philosophical level, but rather were misinterpreted and constructed as signs of an emotional and hysterical woman. Like her heroine, Hays had to struggle to authenticate a subjectivity which was not based primarily on a male conception of female desire.

It may be disappointing to readers to find that after all her struggles, Hays' heroine ultimately becomes a victim, in spite of her capacity for endurance, for resisting the figurative. In *The Wrongs of Woman*, Wollstonecraft begins with the observation: "Was not the world a vast prison, and women born slaves?"[37] When the novel opens, the heroine is already incarcerated by her husband in an asylum. The literalization of the trope of female confinement is immediate, while in Hays' narrative the literalization is deferred. While Hays had used the metaphor of the "magic circle" in her first novel and in her essays,[38] in *Victim of Prejudice* she delays the physical confinement of her heroine. Mary's youthful belief in freedom only renders her powerlessness as an adult more poignant.

Until this final surrender to despair, Mary attempts to find various ways to escape the social and cultural imprisonment of women. Certainly there is pathos in her cry after being raped: "O wretched and ill-fated mother! . . . what calamities has thy frailty entailed upon thy miserable off-spring! Would to God thou hadst never given me exist-ence!" (136–7). While she is presumably addressing her real mother here, the passage could also be read as a plea to Eve, or to a mythical Mother, since she follows it with a didactic warning to "Daughters of levity" (137). Read in the general sense to apply to all women, this becomes a lament for the loss of woman's potential, and seems to suggest an acceptance of those negative qualities tradition-ally associated with the weaker sex. The use of fate in particular seems to be a last resort on Hays' part.

This mournful cry significantly contrasts with Mary's hope at the start. By this time, she feels that from the number of instances of injustice she has experienced, she has "became familiarized, as it were, to suffering." While depicting the realities of the situation of a woman who has lost her "honour," Mary also becomes the quintessen-tial symbol of female suffering. Particularly towards the end, she attains almost sublime stature as the victim, a reminder of the world gone wrong. Like King Lear she responds with five negatives to Osborne's offers of resti-tution: "No, no, no! no more, no more!" (150). Rather heroically, she exclaims that "desolation, infamy, a prison, the rack, death itself" would be preferable to Osborne's overtures (151). Her response is that of a woman driven to extremes because of her lack of choices.

Mary does not, however, give in to death easily. Though Richardson's *Clarissa* is considerably lengthier than Hays' *Victim of Prejudice*, its fictional time is much shorter. Nine months pass between the beginning of Clarissa Harlowe's trials to her death, which occurs about three months after her rape. Mary Raymond's suffering, on the other hand, is protracted to over three years. Af-ter her violation, she spends "six months . . . in occupation

and tranquillity" with her former servant, James (159). After his death, "two tedious years" wear away while Mary
"drag[s] on a joyless existence" (169). Then she spends
another "twelve months" fluctuating "between life and
death" under the Nevilles' care (171). Again, I would argue that deferral here is an effort at resistance. Hays'
attempts to construct a subjectivity for her heroine are
not based on male desire. In other words, unlike that of
Clarissa, Mary's life does not begin and end with her relation to a male figure or lover. Mary may wish to die,
but she does not wither away after the physical assault on
her body. She does establish a kind of pastoral community, however briefly, with James which oversteps the
boundaries of class. The fact that it does not last may
suggest that it is experimental and a merely temporary
solution. But it does show that Hays was still concerned
with the question of female economic and social independence.

In her own life, Hays was to live for more than forty
years after the publication of *Victim of Prejudice*. It remains, however, her strongest polemical feminist piece, as
Hays became much more conservative in the latter half
of her life. As Terence Hoagwood notes, like many writers Hays was driven into "apparent compliance and con-
servatism in the early nineteenth century" by "governmen-
tal and public pressures."[39] To support herself, she published in a variety of genres, including two biographies:
*Female Biography; or, Memoirs of Illustrious and Celebrated
Women, of All Ages and Countries* (1803) and *Memoirs of
Queens Illustrious and Celebrated* (1821). For the most part,
these volumes were not the result of original research,
but were produced through synthesis and compilation of
previously published materials. However, they are attempts to feminize history in their exclusive focus on the

achievements and lives of women. Hays' fiction became increasingly didactic as she grew older. She reworked Henry Brooke's *The Fool of Quality* (1765–70) as *Harry Clinton: A Tale of Youth* in 1804. Joseph Johnson published her *Historical Dialogues for Young Persons* (1806–8) which comprised a series of narratives based on history designed especially for young women. Her last two works of fiction were intended for the education of children of the poor, modelled after Hannah More's popular *Cheap Repository Tracts*. 1815 saw the publication of *The Brothers; or, Consequences. A Story of What Happens Every Day*. Its counterpart, *Family Annals; or, the Sisters* was published in 1817. It appears that Hays published nothing in the last twenty years or so of her life. She died quietly in 1843 at the age of eighty-three.

Parts of this introduction originally appeared in Chapter 3 of *Unsex'd Revolutionaries*. Used by permission of University of Toronto Press.

Notes

1   There has not been much published about Mary Hays to date, but information about her can be found in Gina Luria's, "Mary Hays: A Critical Biography" (Dissertation, New York University, 1972) and more recently, in Gary Kelly's *Women, Writing, and Revolution 1790–1827* (Oxford: Clarendon, 1993).

2   *Analytical Review* 24 (Feb. 1797):174–8; and *Monthly Review* 22 n.s. (April 1797):443–9.

3   *Critical Review* 19 n.s. (Jan. 1797):109–11; and *British Critic* 9 (March 1797):314–5.

4   William Godwin, *Memoirs of the Author of a Vindication of the Rights of Woman*, ed. W. Clark Durant (New York: Haskel House, 1927).

5   For a discussion of the historical and philosophical background of the period, see Marilyn Butler, *Jane Austen and the War of Ideas* (Oxford: Clarendon, 1975; rprnt 1989), and Gary Kelly, *The English Jacobin Novel 1780–1805* (Oxford: Clarendon, 1976).

6   See Eleanor Ty, "Female Philosophy Refunctioned: Elizabeth Hamilton's Parodic Novel," *ARIEL: A Review of International English Literature* 22.4 (Oct. 1991):111–129.

7   See Mary Astell, *A Serious Proposal to the Ladies* (1694) and *A Serious Proposal to the Ladies Part II* (1697); Mary Wollstonecraft, *Thoughts on the Education of Daughters: with Reflections on Female Conduct, in the More Important Duties of Life* (1788); Catherine Macaulay [Graham], *Letters on Education* (1790).

8   Mary Hays, *The Love-Letters of Mary Hays 1779–1780*, ed. A.F. Wedd (London: Methuen, 1925) 219.

9   Mary Hays, *Letters and Essays, Moral and Miscellaneous*, introduction by Gina Luria (New York: Garland, 1974) viii.

10   Mary Hays, *Memoirs of Emma Courtney*, introduction by Sally Cline (London: Pandora, 1987) 31.

11   Hays, *Emma Courtney*, 86.

12   Hays, *Emma Courtney*, 120.

13   Julia Kristeva, "Psychoanalysis and the Polis," in *The Kristeva Reader*, ed. Toril Moi (New York: Columbia UP, 1986) 307.

14   Jane West, *A Gossip's Story and A Legendary Tale*, 2 vols., 4th ed. (London: T.N. Longman & O. Rees, Pater-Noster Row, 1799) II:43.

15   West, *A Gossip's Story*, II:44.

16   See Kelly, *Women, Writing, and Revolution*, chap. 3, and Luria, "Mary Hays," chap. VII.

17   Mary Hays, *Appeal to the Men of Great Britain in Behalf of Women*, introduction by Gina Luria (New York: Garland, 1974) 47.

18   Katharine M. Rogers, "The Contribution of Mary Hays," *Prose Studies* 10.2 (September 1987):132.

19   Kelly, *Women, Writing, and Revolution*, chap. 3.

20   Claudia Johnson, *Jane Austen: Women, Politics, and the Novel* (Chicago: U of Chicago P, 1988) 5.

21   For instance, in Charlotte Smith's *Desmond* (1792), introduction by Gina Luria (New York: Garland, 1974), Geraldine Verney's husband is likened to a tyrant who treats his wife as he would his horses. In the second half of Elizabeth Inchbald's *A Simple Story* (1789), ed. J.M.S. Tompkins (London: Oxford UP, 1967), Lord Elmwood, once priest, then husband, becomes a cruel and harsh father and guardian. For more detailed discussion of these novels, see my book

Unsex'd Revolutionaries: Five Women Novelists of the 1790s (U of Toronto P, 1993).

22 Kelly, *Women, Writing, and Revolution*, chap. 7.

23 Mary Hays, *Memoirs of Queens, Illustrious and Celebrated* (London: T. & J. Allman, 1821) 127.

24 I am influenced by Margaret Homans' views on women and literalization based on Lacan's and Nancy Chodorow's theories. In *Bearing the Word: Language and Female Experience in Nineteenth-Century Women's Writing* (Chicago: U of Chicago P, 1986), Homans argues that a daughter's relation to language is different from that of a son. She associates representational language with the figurative, as it is "symbolic language alone that can approximate the bridging of the gap between child and mother opened up by the. . .prohibition of incest" (7). According to Homans, because of the mother's association with nature, and with the Other, the son tends to "view the mother as literal, she whose absence makes language both necessary and possible" (13). For the daughter, on the other hand, who is "only partially within the symbolic order, the whole question of the literal and the figurative will be more complex" (13). The daughter "will perhaps prefer the literal that her brother devalues" (13), or she "might simply not find the opposition of literal and figurative as telling and important as the son might, for it maintains a boundary not sacred to her—the boundary of the prohibition of incest with the mother" (14).

25 Working with the theories of Klein, Horney, and Deutsch, Marianne Hirsch, in *The Mother/Daughter Plot: Narrative, Psychoanalysis, Feminism* (Bloomington: Indiana UP, 1989),

suggests that narratives of female development "would not be linear or teleological but would reflect the oscillations between maternal and paternal attachments as well as the multiple repressions of the female developmental course" (102).

26 See Jacques Lacan, *Ecrits: A Selection*, trans. Alan Sheridan (New York: Norton, 1977), esp. chap. 6.

27 See Julia Kristeva, *Revolution in Poetic Language*, trans. Margaret Waller, introduction by Leon S. Roudiez (New York: Columbia UP, 1984), esp. chap. I.

Toril Moi, in *Sexual/Textual Politics: Feminist Literary Theory* (London & New York: Methuen, 1985), says that Kristeva's "semiotic *chora* is pre-Oedipal, it is linked to the mother, whereas the symbolic. . . is dominated by the Law of the Father. . . . Kristeva thus delineates two different options for women: mother-identification, which will intensify the pre-Oedipal components of the woman's psyche and render her marginal to the symbolic order, or father-identification, which will create a woman who will derive her identity from the same symbolic order" (164–5).

28 One instance of "bearing the word" that Margaret Homans discusses occurs when the text "performs linguistic operations—translation, transmission, copying" of the language of other authors (*Bearing the Word*, p. 3). Here Hays does not actually "bear the word" of another, but she does replicate her own story or fears.

29 For example, Charlotte Smith's *Emmeline, or the Orphan of the Castle* (1788), Ann Radcliffe's *The Mysteries of Udolpho* (1794), and Elizabeth Inchbald's *A Simple Story* (1791) featured abducted maidens. However, in these novels the

heroines escape before they are actually violated.

30 M.H., "On Novel Writing," *The Monthly Magazine* (September 1797):180.

31 *The Monthly Magazine*, p. 180.

32 See Homans, *Bearing the Word*, pp. 4ff

33 Mary Wollstonecraft, *Mary and The Wrongs of Woman* (Oxford: World's Classics, 1976) 106, 109.

34 In *Speculum of the Other Woman*, trans. Gillian C. Gill (Ithaca: Cornell UP, 1985), Luce Irigaray claims that as subjects, males project their desires onto the "Other." Subjectivity is "denied to woman;" she functions as "a mirror to catch his reflection" (133–4). In Margaret Whitford's words, "Irigaray argues. . . that all of western discourse and culture displays the structure of specularization, in which the male projects his own ego on to the world, which then becomes a mirror which enables him to see his own reflection wherever he looks." {Luce Irigary: *Philosophy in the Feminine* (New York: Routledge, 1991) 34.}

35 Luria, "Mary Hays," 400.

36 Charles Lamb, *The Letters of Charles and Mary Anne Lamb*, vol. I: 1796–1801, ed. Edwin W. Marrs, Jr. (Ithaca: Cornell UP, 1975), 182.

37 Wollstonecraft, *Mary and the Wrongs of Woman*, 79.

38 See Explanatory Notes, 39, 47

39   Terence Allan Hoagwood, Introduction to *Victim of Preju-dice* by Mary Hays (New York: Scholars' Facsimiles & Re-prints, 1990), 9.

Note on the Text

This text is that of the two volume edition published by Joseph Johnson in 1799. The long 's' has been modernized, and the running quotation marks eliminated. Idiosyncrasies of punctuation and inconsistencies in spelling have been left untouched as they conform to acceptable eighteenth-century usage. Hays' notes, indicated by asterisks, are retained at the foot of the page; editorial notes, indicated by numbers in superscript, are placed at the end of the text.

THE
VICTIM
OF
PREJUDICE.

IN TWO VOLUMES.

BY MARY HAYS,

AUTHOR OF

THE MEMOIRS OF EMMA COURTNEY.

VOL. I.

Her Trumpet Slander rais'd on high,
And told the Tidings to the Sky;
Contempt discharg'd a living Dart,
A side-long Viper, to her Heart;
Reproach breath'd Poisons o'er her Face,
And soil'd and blasted ev'ry Grace;
Officious Shame, her Handmaid new,
Still turn'd the Mirror to her View;
While those, in Crimes the deepest dy'd,
Approach'd to whiten at her Side.

Moore's Female Seducers.

LONDON:

PRINTED FOR J. JOHNSON, ST. PAUL'S CHURCH-YARD.

1799.

Advertisement to the Reader

IN A FORMER PUBLICATION,[2] I endeavoured to inculcate an important lesson, by exemplifying the errors of sensibility, or the pernicious consequences of indulged passion, even in a mind of no common worth and powers. To avoid, as I conceived, the possibility of misconstruction, I spoke of my heroine, in the preface, not as an *example*, but as a *warning*: yet the cry of slander was raised against me;[3] I was accused of recommending those excesses, of which I laboured to paint the disastrous effects. Lest dullness or malignity should again wrest my purpose, it may be necessary to premise, that, in delineating, in the following pages, the mischiefs which have ensued the too-great stress laid on the *reputation* for chastity[4] in *woman*, no disrespect is intended to this most important branch of temperance, the cement, the support, and the bond, of social-virtue: it is the *means* only, which are used to ensure it, that I presume to call in question. *Man* has hitherto been solicitous at once to indulge his own voluptuousness and to counteract its baneful tendencies: not less tragical than absurd have been the consequences! They may be traced in the corruption of our youth; in the dissoluteness which, like a flood, has overspread the land; in the sacrifice of hecatombs of victims. Let *man* revert to the source of these evils; let him be chaste

1

himself, nor seek to reconcile contradictions. — Can the streams run pure while the fountain is polluted?

Introduction

A CHILD OF MISFORTUNE, a wretched outcast from my fellow-beings, driven with ignominy from social intercourse, cut off from human sympathy, immured in the gloomy walls of a prison,[5] I spread my hands and lift my eyes to the Moral Governor of the Universe! If, as I have been taught to believe, a Being existeth, who searcheth the heart, and judgeth not as man judgeth,[6] to Him I make my last appeal from the injustice and barbarity of society.

And thou, the victim of despotism, oppression, or error, tenant of a dungeon,[7] and successor to its present devoted inhabitant, should these sheets fall into thy possession, when the hand that wrote them moulders in the dust, and the spirit that dictated ceases to throb with indignant agony, read; and, if civil refinements have not taught thy heart to reflect the sentiment which cannot penetrate it, spare from the contemplation of thy own misery one hour, and devote it to the memory of a fellow-sufferer, who derives firmness from innocence, courage from despair; whose unconquerable spirit, bowed but not broken, seeks to beguile, by the retrospect of an unsullied life, the short interval, to which will succeed a welcome and never-ending repose.

The Victim of Prejudice

[Volume I]

Chapter I

IN THE FIRST DAWNINGS of infant sensibility,[8] the earliest recollections which I have of my being, I found myself healthful, sportive, happy, residing in a romantic village in the county of Monmouthshire,[9] under the protection of Mr. Raymond, a sensible and benevolent man, a little advanced beyond the middle period of life, who, for some years past, had retreated from the pursuits of a gay and various life, and, with the small remnant of an originally-moderate fortune, had secluded himself in a rural and philosophic retirement.

To the wisdom and kindness of my benefactor, who, with a contempt of vulgar prejudices, cherished notions somewhat singular respecting female accomplishments, I was indebted for a robust constitution, a cultivated understanding, and a vigorous intellect.[10] I was early inured to habits of hardiness; to suffer, without shrinking, the changes and inclemencies of the seasons; to endure fatigue and occasional labour; to exercise my ingenuity and exert my faculties, arrange my thoughts and discipline my imagination. At ten years of age, I could ride the forest-horses without bridle or saddle; could leap a fence or surmount a gate with admirable dexterity; could climb the highest trees, wrestle with the children of the village, or mingle in the dance with grace and activity. Tall, blooming, animated, my features were regular, my complexion a rich glowing brunette, my eyes vivacious and sparkling; dark chestnut hair shaded my face, and floated over my shoulders in luxuriant profusion; my figure was light and airy, my step firm, my aspect intelligent, and my mind inquisitive.

The modest and candid reader will excuse this seeming vanity in the description of my personal accomplishments, when informed, that the graces, with which nature had so liberally endowed me, proved a material link in the chain of events,[11] that led to the subsequent incidents of my life; a life embittered by unrelenting persecution, and marked by undeserved calamities; the measure of which appears at length to be filled up.

Mr. Raymond instructed me in the rudiments of the French, Italian, and Latin, languages; in the elements of geometry, algebra, and arithmetic.[12] I drew problems, calculated abstract quantities, and learned to apply my principles to astronomy, and other branches of natural knowledge. The instructions of my tutor were communicated with so much kindness, my studies were so blended with amusement, so little restraint was laid upon the freedom of my humour, or the wild simplicity of my age, that my lessons, my exercises, and my sports, seemed but diversified sources of pleasure and amusement.

Ignorant respecting the authors or the circumstances of my birth, I felt too happy and too careless to make them subjects of inquiry. Mr. Raymond, to my young and ardent imagination, appeared at once my parent, protector, and tutelar deity. I bounded into his arms after every short absence; I knew no transport equal to that afforded me by his smiles and caresses, and prattled to him without apprehension or disguise; I was unacquainted with fear, and comprehended neither the nature of, nor the temptations to, falsehood.

Chapter II

I HAD SCARCELY COMPLETED my eleventh year, when my benefactor was prevailed upon, by the importunity of a friend, to undertake the tuition of two youths, heirs to a gentleman of an ancient family and ample fortune; who, desirous of bestowing upon them a liberal education, dreaded to expose their morals to the contagion of a great school. Some embarrassments of a pecuniary nature assisted in determining my patron, whose spirit had not always confined itself within the limits of his income, to accede the more readily to the proposal of his friend, and preparations were made for the accommodation of this addition to our little household. Every thing, which, at an early period of life, promises novelty, is attractive. Rejoicing in the anticipation of this accession to our family, I waited impatiently for the hour that would bring me new associates in my studies and companions in my sports.

The wished-for period at length arrived, when the Honourable Mr. Pelham, followed by his sons, William and Edmund, alighted from a post-coach[13] at the entrance of our rural habitation. Being with Mr. Raymond in his study, on the introduction of our guests, I scrutinized with a lively curiosity their manners and appearance. Mr. Pelham seemed to me to be about the middle period of life, some years younger than my guardian; his carriage was stately and solemn, his air cold and reserved. William, the elder of the youths, was in his thirteenth year; tall, well-proportioned, handsome, active, bold, and spirited. Edmund, younger by several years than his brother, was sickly and delicate, his voice feeble, his countenance amiable, and his manners mild and gentle.

Some preliminary discourse ensued between Mr. Raymond and his guest, respecting the abilities and future destination of the lads; who were by no means to degrade a long and illustrious line of ancestry by the practice of any profession or commercial employment. Mr. Pelham summed up his directions, by adding emphatically, that, above all things, it must be the care of the preceptor to preserve his charge from forming any improper acquaintance, or humiliating connections, which might tend to interfere with his views for their future dignity and advancement. The family honour, he informed my patron, had been preserved uncontaminated for many generations, and it was his pride that it should descend unsullied to posterity.

The meaning of these expressions I by no means comprehended on their delivery, but various circumstances have since but too frequently recalled them to my recollection, and impressed them upon my feelings in characters never to be effaced. Mr. Pelham, during his stay, which was till the ensuing morning, scarcely honoured me with his notice, excepting by a slight inquiry if I was the daughter of his host.

"No, sir," replied my friend, "I have not the happiness of calling this lovely girl mine, except by adoption. She is an unfortunate orphan, whom it is equally my duty and my delight to shelter from a world that will hardly be inclined to do her justice, and upon which she has few claims."

There was something in the tone of Mr. Raymond's voice, while he thus expressed himself, that thrilled through my heart with a new and indescribable sensation. The awe with which I had been impressed by the presence of his guest gave way to a more powerful and irresistible emotion; throwing my arms round the neck of my benefactor, I burst into tears, and sobbed upon his bosom.

Equally surprised and affected by this sudden transport, he gently soothed me; while, to divert the passion he had unwarily excited, he proposed that I should accompany the young gentlemen into the garden, and shew them our collection of botanical plants. For the first time in my life, I had been sensible to an embarrassment, and a temporary feeling of depression and apprehension; a prelude, as it should seem, to those anxieties and sorrows which have since pursued me with unmitigated severity, against which I have vainly struggled, and whose overwhelming consequences I am no longer able to combat or evade.

Withdrawing myself from the arms of my patron, I breathed a heavy sigh. He kissed the tear from my glowing cheek, while his meek eyes beamed with kindness. I accepted his commission with alacrity, pleased to be delivered from the presence of Mr. Pelham, whose austere manners chilled my spirits, and suspended the light and joyous sensations, which, till that inauspicious moment, had converted every little incident of my life into a new source of pleasure and entertainment. Relieved from the constraint imposed by the behaviour of his father, William, taking my hand, and gazing in my face with an expression of lively sympathy, addressed me in kind and encouraging accents. We proceeded, followed by his brother, to the garden, where the impressions from the preceding scene were quickly forgotten. We laughed, wrestled, romped, contended in various sports and feats of activity, in the boldness and agility of which I emulated my companion, while my daring stimulated him to greater exertion. If I found myself foiled by his superior strength and stature, yet, in courage, in spirit, in dexterity, and resource, he was compelled to acknowledge he had met with no contemptible rival.

In a short time, from a mutual display of congenial qualities and an interchange of kindness, we became thoroughly impressed with affection for each other. Enjoying the present, and anticipating the future, with the light and sanguine spirits of youth, I forgot, in the society of the son, the painful feelings inspired by the presence of the father. Edmund, whom infirm health had, by its enfeebling effects, prevented from participating in our sports, seemed, nevertheless, exhilarated by our gambols, and caught, from sympathy, a portion of the hilarity of which he was incapacitated from taking a more active share.

Chapter III

A GENEROUS EMULATION inspired me with redoubled ardour in the pursuit of my studies. William, with quick perceptions and a vigorous imagination, was careless, dissipated, fond of pleasure, and averse to application: Edmund, with a mind and temperament less active and lively, outstripped, by habits more attentive and persevering, the progress of his brother. While the gentle Edmund interested my sympathy, and inspired me with tenderness, the warm affections, lively feelings, and enterprising spirit, of William were better suited to my habits and temper. In the hours of amusement, we became inseparable; we seemed animated but by one heart and one mind; we took our lessons together; and, when (a case by no means unfrequent) William loitered in his exercises or left his task unfinished, I redoubled my diligence and application, that I might have leisure to assist him. Mr. Raymond perceived with pleasure the harmony which subsisted between us, and encouraged us in reciprocal acts of sympathy and kindness: regarding youth as the proper season for the cultivation of social affections, he delighted in observing the guileless and innocent testimonies of friendship which we mutually manifested and received. The disposition of William was somewhat impetuous, impatient of control, and liable to sudden gusts of passion; yet these emotions were transient; his impressions, more lively than permanent, readily yielded to new objects and new occurrences. An incident which occurred at this period, though in itself trifling, is too characteristic to be omitted.

The lord of the manor, who resided not far from our cottage, was particularly curious[14] in his shrubs and fruit-trees, and we were strictly prohibited from trespassing, on any pretence or occasion, on his premises. Sauntering, one fine summer's evening, near the park-palings, we observed, within the enclosure, but not far distant, an open green-house, from the windows of which hung a large and tempting cluster of grapes, of uncommon ripeness, bloom, and beauty.

"Mary," said William, taking my hand, and pointing to the forbidden fruit, "I have a great inclination to procure some of those grapes that hang so invitingly. What say you? should you not like, this warm evening, to partake a refreshment so cooling and delicious?"

"No, no, William," replied I, averting my eyes from the luscious bait, "you know my father," (so was I accustomed to call my dear benefactor,) "who never restricts us unreasonably, has, on this subject, given us a particular caution."

"Mr. Raymond is over scrupulous," rejoined William, reddening, and quickening his pace. "And you," added he, leering slily in my face, "like the rest of your weak sex, are timid and spiritless."

"Is this kind, William? Is it just?"

"Well, but, Mary, I have a strange fancy for those grapes. I wish also that you should share them with me. Your father will know nothing about the matter, unless we should be silly enough to betray ourselves."

"But suppose he should hear of it, and question me on the subject; I never yet concealed any thing from him; and I could not tell a falsehood" (in a softened voice) "even for *you*, William."

"Foolish girl! he loves you too well, and you know it, to be angry with you."

"Ah, William, is that a reason why I should venture to displease him?"

"Your friendship for me is weak, since you will hazard

nothing to oblige me."

"But *you*, also, will incur his displeasure, William."

"I care not; it is enough, I have given up the point In future, I shall better know how to make an estimate of your courage and affection."

Saying which, he turned from me, apparently disgusted, and was presently out of sight. I remained, for some moments, involved in a train of reflections, equally painful and perplexing. The unkind and petulant reproaches of William had pierced my heart: he had also questioned my courage. This I could have submitted to; but had he not likewise affected to doubt my *love?* — I paced backward and forward, agitated by contending feelings. Should I violate almost the only injunction of my indulgent patron? Should I add to that violation the meanness of concealment or evasion? My eyes filled with tears, and my bosom palpitated. Should I expose myself to detection from the squire and his family, and suffer the imputation of gluttony and trespass? An indignant glow suffused my cheek. But, then, what a sweet compensation would the consciousness afford, that it was not for selfish gratification I had subjected myself to hazard and censure, but to serve and oblige my friend. The difficulties and possible mortifications attending the enterprise would but enhance its value; I should prove, at once, my spirit and my affection: the risk, too, would be all mine; the absence of William must exonerate him from blame, and his share in the transaction might rest in my own bosom: to Edmund, also, whom the fervour of the weather has rendered feverish and indisposed, how refreshing and grateful would be this delicious fruit. The last consideration fixed the wavering balance, and confirmed my resolution. To a young casuist these reasonings bore a specious appearance: assuming the respectable forms of generosity and tenderness, they dazzled, and finally prevailed.

With some difficulty, I surmounted the fence, and proceeded boldly towards the green-house. Having seized and secured the tempting bait, I was about to retreat with the spoil, when a burst of mirth from behind a thicket, accompanied with loud shoutings, suspended my steps, and fixed me motionless with surprise. I held in my hand the proof of my guilt, the consciousness of which shook my frame with a trepidation to which it had been little accustomed. A tumultuous party of young men issued from a grove, and advanced hastily towards me: I attempted not to fly, but, rallying my spirits, firmly waited their approach.

"Ah! my little lass," cried the foremost, seizing me, "have we caught you in the fact?[15] – Detection, upon my soul!" (attempting to snatch the fruit, which I resolutely grasped:) "a true daughter of Eve!"

As I struggled to disengage myself from his hold, a large straw hat, which shaded my face from the sun, fell back, and, suspended by the riband, hung upon my shoulders; over which, my dishevelled hair streamed in wild disorder.

Starting backward a few paces, and staring rudely in my face, "By God!" said he, "a little beauty! a Hebe![16] a wood-nymph! I must and will have a kiss; and, d—n me! you shall be welcome to all the grapes in the green-house."

Shocked and frightened by a brutality of manner so novel and unexpected, with a sudden spring I evaded his grasp, and, winged by terror and disgust, flew towards the boundaries of the park with inconceivable swiftness. Having distanced my pursuers, and scrambled over the fence, with my clothes torn, my hands and arms bruised, scratched, and streaming with blood, I rushed towards the dear and well-known asylum, the peaceful mansion of my revered benefactor, still retaining in my hand the fatal cause of my fault and of my terror. On the threshold of our cottage I encountered Mr. Raymond, accompanied by his pupils. Panting, breathless, heated by the fervour of the weather, flushed by the consciousness of guilt, and exhausted by perturbation and fatigue, I ran into his arms, that seemed to open spontaneously to receive me.

"Mary! my child!" exclaimed my more than father, in an accent of solicitude and alarm. "why this terror, this agitation? What has injured, what has befallen, my child?"

Unable to reply, my head sunk on my bosom, while a few tears, forcing their way, stole down my burning cheek. Disengaging myself from the arms of my friend, I perceived William, whose countenance manifested evident signs of confusion, gliding from the presence of his tutor, and stealing gently into the house. I started; and, precipitately advancing towards him, put into his hands the fruit I had so dearly purchased.

"What means all this?" interrogated Mr. Raymond. "Whence came those grapes? Why do you give them to William?"

"They came, sir," (I dared not call him by the endearing name of father,) "from the green-house of Sir Peter Osborne: I give them to William, because — *I love him.*"

William blushed, and hung his head.

"Explain yourself, my child! You speak in enigmas."

"I have nothing more to say, sir."

"Who gave you the fruit? and how know you that it belonged to Sir Peter Osborne?"

"No person gave it to me; I took it myself."

"How! what! took it yourself! is it possible? How did you gain access to the green-house?"

"I climbed over the fence, and plucked the grapes, which hung from an open casement."

Mr. Raymond appeared petrified with astonishment.

"Who saw you? Whence came this blood? Who has wounded you and torn your clothes? How came you in this condition?"

"I was discovered by some gentlemen, whom the trees had concealed from me. One of them seized and terrified me: I escaped from his hands; and, in my haste to regain the road, bruised and tore myself."

While I thus artlessly replied to the inquiries of my friend, I ventured not to lift my eyes to his: a confused consciousness of my fault flashed upon my mind, depriving it of its wonted confidence.

"Well, Mary," resumed he, and sighed, "you have now only to give me a recital of the motives which influenced you to this extraordinary step, with the same ingenuousness with which you have already related the transaction and its consequences. I confess, I know not how to suspect you of gluttony: did you mean to eat these grapes?"

"No, sir."

"Was it merely to present them to William that you subjected yourself to a situation thus painful and humiliating?"

I blushed, trembled, and was silent.

"Did William require of you this sacrifice?"

"No, sir."

"I perceive," replied he, coldly, "you are not inclined to give me satisfaction on this subject. I wish not to *extort* your confidence."

My heart swelled almost to bursting; but I restrained its emotions. I shed no tears; my downcast eyes remained fixed upon the ground. Cold shiverings seized me, which were in a few minutes succeeded by a burning heat. My lungs seemed oppressed; a pain darted through my temples; I respired with difficulty. Mr. Raymond, coming towards me, took my hand: the pulse throbbed beneath his fingers.

"Poor child!" said he, in a tone of concern, "you are in a high fever; you have overheated your blood."

Leading me into the house, he delivered me to the care of the housekeeper, who retired with me to my chamber. I passed a restless night; and, towards morning, became much worse. In the course of the ensuing day, the symptoms appeared sufficiently threatening to fill my benefactor with serious apprehension, and induce him to call in medical aid. The physician pronounced my disorder to be a scarlet fever, which had lately been prevalent in the neighbouring hamlet.

In the mean time, scarcely quitting my apartment, Mr. Raymond watched every turn of my disease, treating me with the most soothing tenderness. This kindness gave an additional pang to my heart: I felt myself unworthy of his goodness; and, by the struggles of my mind, increased the violence of my distemper. On the third day, the fever abated, and my disorder began to assume a more favourable aspect. My dear patron testified the most lively joy, but I was still far from being reconciled to myself.

My young companions, I was informed, had, to preserve them from infection, been removed to a neighbouring farm-house, and strictly interdicted from approaching our habitation.

On the fifth day of my indisposition, while reclining on a sopha, in a small room that looked towards the garden, whither I had been removed for the benefit of the air, Mr. Raymond having just retired to his study, the door suddenly flew open, when William, rushing in, threw himself upon my neck, and, tenderly embracing me, burst into a passion of tears.

"Ah, my dear Mary!" cried he, in a voice interrupted

by sobs, "I can never pardon myself the sufferings I have occasioned you. I was determined to see you and implore your forgiveness, nor should all the world have prevented me."

As he thus spoke, my patron, alarmed at hearing an unusual noise in the apartment, from which his study was not far distant, re-entered. I had disengaged myself, with features expressing consternation and horror, from the embraces of William.

"Take him away!" exclaimed I, clasping my hands together in an agony, and trying to avoid him. "Oh, take him away! He will catch the fever; he will be sick and die; and, then, what will become of Mary!"

Mr. Raymond advanced with a serious and resolute aspect. William sunk upon his knees.

"Tell her, sir," said he passionately, "that I have confessed all the truth, that I repent of my folly and wickedness, and shall never be happy till I have obtained her and your forgiveness."

His tutor, without reply, led him from the room; and, giving him in charge to a servant, to be reconducted to the farm, returned to me.

"What uneasiness," said he, on entering, "has this rash boy occasioned us! I feared to mention the subject to my little girl," (tenderly taking my hands in his,) "lest, in her weak state, it might have given her disturbance; but let me now assure her, that her conduct in the affair, though certainly imprudent and not entirely blameless, has nevertheless endeared her to my heart with, if possible, a thousand additional ties."

I threw myself into his arms, and wept aloud, — delicious tears of reconciliation and grateful affection:

he wiped them with his handkerchief, kissed me tenderly, and, artfully changing the subject, gradually soothed and tranquillized my spirits.

Chapter IV

I HAD SCARCELY RECOVERED from the effects of my indisposition, when William, sickening, discovered evident signs of infection. Mr. Raymond, alarmed by these appearances, after having again removed Edmund, sent an express to Mr. Pelham, with an account of the situation of his son. Mr. Pelham returned with the messenger. On his arrival, the eruption had appeared, attended with threatening symptoms. During many days, the event was doubtful: we fluctuated alternately between hope and fear. I could scarcely be torn from the apartment, to take necessary rest and refreshment: William would receive nothing but from my hands, while I wept incessantly over sufferings I was unable to alleviate.

At length, the disorder took a favourable turn. William daily acquired health and strength; his father, every apprehension of danger being now removed, returned to town; and, in a few weeks, no other consequences remained of the malady than a slight degree of languor and weakness.

This incident, which I regarded as a grateful proof of his affection, added to the remembrance of his sufferings on my account, served but to endear him to me yet more tenderly. I redoubled my cares and efforts to oblige and amuse him.

As the health of William became entirely re-established, we returned to our sports and occupations with renewed spirits and glee.

One fine autumnal morning, rambling through the fields, just after sun-rise, as was our custom, we heard the cry of the dogs and the shouts of the hunters. We ran, with youthful curiosity, towards a lane whence the mingled sounds, returned by the echoes, seemed to proceed.

We had scarcely reached the place, when a hare, panting, breathless, and limping, rushed past us, and fell, a few paces distant, to the ground. I flew towards the distressed animal, and, thoughtless of my danger, threw myself beside it on the turf, endeavouring to shelter it with my feeble arms. The dogs advanced in full cry; I shrieked; William ran to my assistance, when the huntsman, suddenly appearing in sight from a winding of the lane, and observing our perilous situation, called off the eager animals, who were within a short distance of their trembling, defenceless, prey. Some gentlemen riding up, one of them loudly cried to us to quit the hare, while the poor animal, his sides palpitating, seemed to look wistfully in my face, as if imploring protection. My heart melted with compassion: I hovered still more closely over the panting victim, disdaining any reply to his savage persecutors. The gentleman, leaping from his horse, advanced towards me; when William, intercepting, dared to oppose him. Brandishing his horse-whip, he threatened to exercise it upon my friend, when, starting from the ground, and rushing between them, I received several smart strokes, designed for William, over my neck and shoulders. The remainder of the company now interposed.

"For shame, Sir Peter!" said a gentleman, who, having alighted from his horse, hastened to my relief: "do not exert this unmanly rage against defenceless children: the humanity, courage, and spirit, of this little lass deserve better treatment."

"D—n me," replied the keen sportsman, "am I to have my sport interrupted by a peasant's brats?"

As his friend held his arm, perceiving William no longer in danger, I returned to my charge, who, exhausted by fatigue, was unable to escape from the spot on which it had sunk. My neck and arms bore marks of the rough discipline I had received, yet I neither uttered a complaint nor shed a tear: indignation inspired me with a sullen fortitude; while, in the smart of blows acquired in the cause of humanity and friendship, I found only a source of triumph. The whole party, having by this time alighted, surrounded us, when my adversary, after staring for some moments rudely in my face, shouted in a discordant tone,

"May I be d—ned if this is not the little thief that stole the grapes from the green-house? By G-d! my pretty dear! you shall not escape me now; but shall pay the full forfeit of all your trespasses."

Saying which, he seized me, and, clasping me in his arms, kissed me with an odious violence. I shrieked, struggled, and fought, with all my strength. William, seeing me so freely and roughly treated, snatched the whip of my persecutor, which, in the contest, had fallen to the ground, and assaulted him with fury. Obliged to relinquish his prey, he turned to defend himself from the attack of my champion, whom his companions, with difficulty, released from his vengeance. The gentleman who had at first been my advocate again interposed.

"I insist upon it, Sir Peter," said he, in a resolute tone of voice, "that you commit no more violence upon these young people, who have given you no serious cause of offence, and whom I am determined to protect."

After some altercation, peace was restored, we were permitted to depart, and the hare was, by the general voice of the company, awarded to me, as a recompense for my courage and sufferings in its defence.

Mr. Raymond, to whom our unusual absence had occasioned some solicitude, met us on our return. William related circumstantially to him all that had passed. Regarding me with looks of affectionate concern and interest, he applauded my spirit and humanity, repeatedly pressing me to his heart. There was an affecting solemnity in his voice and manner that struck upon my spirits. He sighed frequently, as he gazed upon the marks which the discipline of the whip had inflicted, and turned from me, as if to hide a starting tear.

"I do not mind them," said I, observing his concern. "Have you not taught me, dear father, that, in the cause of *right* we should contemn bodily pain?[17] Besides," (clasping my hands together with an animated gesture,) "I rejoice in these scars; were they not blows intercepted from William?"

Mr. Raymond, apparently overcome by an emotion that would no longer be controlled, quitted us precipitately.

Chapter V

BY THESE LITTLE INCIDENTS, the innocent and growing tenderness between myself and my youthful companion was increased and cemented. For the first time, reflections occurred to the mind of my benefactor that occasioned him some uneasiness: yet, he was too wise to risk, by any premature hint or precaution, the giving a reality to what, at present, he hoped was but a chimerical evil.

The animal we had rescued from the sportsmen was, by our care and assiduities, in a short time restored to health and vigour.

"Let us give him freedom," said I to William, who proposed to restrain him. "Liberty, my father has told me, is the truest and most invaluable good. He has no longer need of our assistance: he would pine with us while sequestered from his fellows and companions: let us not be more barbarous than the savages who would have shed his blood."

To the justice of these reasonings William assented, and we restored our happy and bounding captive to his native woods.

These incidents had impressed me with a horror for the name and character of Sir Peter Osborne, whose grounds and their environs I cautiously avoided.

Happy in the society of my young companions, time glided swiftly away in a thousand varied pleasures. We continued to improve in stature and in knowledge: we received our lessons in common. The feeble health of Edmund was an impediment to his acquirements: William's gaiety and dissipation interrupted his application. I outstripped both my companions: with an active mind and an ardent curiosity, I conceived an enthusiastic love of science and literature.[18] Mr. Raymond directed my attention, encouraged my emulation, and afforded me the most liberal assistance.

Mr. Pelham occasionally recalled his sons, to make short visits to his house in London. During their absence, my vivacity forsook me and my spirits languished. On their return, William and I bounded into each other's embraces; while, all life, spirit, and gaiety, we laughed and prattled, eagerly related the little occurrences of our separation, and, in the joyous present and anticipated future, forgot the anxieties and vexations of the past.

William at length entered into his nineteenth, and I into my seventeenth, year. Tall, healthful, glowing, my person already began to display all the graces and the bloom of womanhood: my understanding was cultivated and mature, but my heart simple and guileless, my temper frank, and my manners wild and untutored. My benefactor had, for some time past, anxiously watched the growing attachment between myself and his pupil. He, deeply regretted the painful necessity of checking a sympathy at once so natural, virtuous, and amiable. He knew not how to debauch the simplicity of my mind by acquainting me with the manners and maxims of the world. How could he, to my unsophisticated understanding, explain the motives which influenced his conduct? or, unfolding them, how be able to repel my artless, but just, reasoning? Painful suspicions assailed him: he began to doubt whether, in cultivating my mind, in fostering a virtuous sensibility, in imbuing my heart with principles of justice and rectitude, he had not been betraying my happiness! — Gracious God! what must be the habits of society, which could give rise to such an apprehension? An apprehension, alas! which, in these embittered moments, I feel but too much inclined to believe verified. *Prudence* seems no longer to be under-

THE VICTIM OF PREJUDICE

stood in its just and original signification, — The wise government of our inordinate desires, a graceful regard to the propriety of our actions, a rational and dignified self-respect: in its stead has been substituted a sordid calculation of self-interest, a bigotted attachment to forms and semblances, a persevering suppression of every generous, every ardent, every amiable, affection, that should threaten to interfere with our baser and more sinister views.

Chapter VI

ONE EVENING, after passing the day with William in our usual lively affectionate intercourse, Mr. Raymond sent for me in his study. I obeyed his summons with alacrity, and, on entering, ran towards him with the lightness of spirit with which I had been accustomed to conform myself to his most indifferent requests. He appeared not to receive me with his usual cheerfulness; an expression of perplexity sat upon his features, while a cloud hung over his brow. My spirits caught the alarm.

"My father!" said I, in an accent of anxiety and concern, taking his hand, and looking tenderly in his face; "you are not well. What has discomposed you? Speak to me. Can I do nothing to serve or relieve you?"

"Sit down, my love! Nothing has happened: I am not ill; I merely wish to have a little conversation with you."

"Ah!" kissing his hands alternately, "have I been so unhappy as to displease you? Do let me know my error, that I may instantly repair it."

"You never displeased me; you are incapable of displeasing me: I know of no fault which you have, unless it be an excess of goodness. The concern which I feel at present arises solely from the fear that I shall be compelled to wound the gentle nature of my beloved girl."

"Go on, dear sir; I am satisfied, you cannot exact from me what is unreasonable, you cannot demand of me more than I will cheerfully perform."

Clasping me to his breast, he embraced me with paternal kindness. "I have been to blame to alarm you by this solemnity; there is no cause for it;" (and he affected to smile;) "your delicacy and your quickness will lead you readily to comprehend the motives which oblige me to

27

require of you what may, at first, perhaps, appear a sacrifice somewhat painful."

I gazed on him with a mixture of astonishment, curiosity, and solicitude. He proceeded, after a few moments hesitation.

"You are now, my dear Mary, approaching towards womanhood: I behold the loveliness of your person and the graces of your mind with all a parent's partial fondness, but with all a parent's anxiety. Your own excellent understanding will suggest to you, that propriety of action varies at different periods of life; that our social and relative duties are perpetually changing, and, as they change, suggest to us distinct modes of conduct. The first and most earnest purpose of my cares and precepts has been, by forming you to virtue, to secure your *happiness*: for this *end*, I have laboured to awaken, excite, and strengthen, your mind. An enlightened intellect is the highest of human endowments; it affords us an inexhaustible source of power, dignity, and enjoyment. 'Of extraordinary talents, like diamonds of uncommon magnitude, it has been truly said, calculation cannot find the value.'[*19] Their favoured possessors are the genuine sovereigns of mankind: they direct, they model, they govern, the world. But I will not try to conceal from you, that the vivid sensations, exquisite sensibilities, powerful energies, and imperious passions,[20] which necessarily accompany superior mental excellence, have but too frequently, when habits of self-government and independence of mind have not been early and assiduously cultivated, served but to betray the possessor, to plunge him into deeper and more deplorable ruin, to gild the wreck over which humanity weeps and trembles. Poisons the most deadly are produced amidst the luxurious vegetation of the tropics: compared with the lion of the African desert, in strength, in size, in ferocity, the

* Holcroft's *Anna St. Ives* [Hays' note]

savage animal who inhabits the northern wilderness is tame and powerless."

"I perceive, with pride and pleasure, the vigorous promise of your blossoming faculties; I rejoice that my efforts have not been fruitless, that my speculations have not proved an idle theory, nor my plans and expectations a philosophic dream: yet the highest and the proudest boast of genius were vain, but as a *mean* to an *end*. If I have not secured your happiness and rendered you useful to society; if I have not taught you to subdue yourself, to subject your feelings, to direct your views steadily to objects worthy of your attention, to contemn the suggestions of a near and partial interest, to triumph over the imperious demands of passion,[21] to yield only to the dictates of right reason and truth; my cares have indeed been worthless and my efforts vain: infinitely more enviable will be the lot of the peasant, who, toiling ceaseless through the day, draws from the sterile earth a scanty sustenance, satisfies the cravings of nature, and reposes in the hovel of indigence; who has neither leisure to feel, nor capacity to comprehend, the multiplied sources of anguish from which the shafts of disappointment draw their deadly venom, while they transfix and rankle in the tender and susceptible heart."

My benefactor paused here: his face glowed; his tones were unusually touching, they thrilled through my nerves: he looked wistfully in my face: his eyes were moist with tears, yet illumined with a benign lustre; their mild and penetrating rays seemed to pervade my soul. Grasping his hand, I had sunk unconsciously upon my knees before him, and, while I eagerly examined his features, caught every accent as it proceeded from his lips. My bosom throbbed responsively to the sentiments which he uttered: I held in my breath, lest I should interrupt or lose a single syllable: I felt animated as by a divine enthusiasm, my thoughts elevated, my mind expanded. For some minutes after he ceased to speak, I continued to gaze, to listen; every faculty of my soul absorbed, wrapt in attention. Raising me from the ground, he gently re-seated me: I clasped my hands, and exclaimed with fervour,

"Name the sacrifice you require; distrust not the mind you have formed; your dictates and those of *reason* are the same, they have ever been uniform and invariable. Behold me, my father, resigned to your will!"

Mr. Raymond rose, visibly affected, and traversed the room with a quick, but unequal, pace. At length, turning towards me,

"It is I, my dear Mary," said he, "who want firmness, who am unable to give an example of the fortitude I would fain inculcate. Your artless, your affectionate eloquence unnerves me. How shall I tell you that I doubt I must, for a time, rob myself of the joy of my life, the tender attentions, caresses, and society, of my little girl. Yes, it is, I feel, but too necessary that we should separate, for days, for months, perhaps for years."

I started, trembled, shuddered; I felt a sudden revulsion of blood and spirits; in a moment my face was bathed in tears. Seizing the hand of my benefactor, I wept bitterly.

"What have I done?" cried I passionately, in a voice interrupted by sobs, "that I must be exiled from your presence? Whom have I in the world but you and William? Ah! you will soon cease to be troubled with an unhappy orphan; I shall not long survive when banished from you!"

Yielding to the first burst of feeling, my patron folded me in his arms, and shed over me a flood of tears. His manly spirit for a time vainly contended with his emotions, till, making a strenuous effort, he struggled with

and subdued himself, assumed an aspect of more composure, and gently soothed my distress, till I became gradually resigned and tranquil.

"It is from *William*," resumed Mr. Raymond, in a severer tone, "that I think it prudent to separate you." A
convulsive tremor shook my frame: — without seeming to
remark my emotion, he proceeded. "I will not deceive
you, my child, by false and feeble pretences. With the
purity and the simplicity of your heart I am well acquainted. The mutual harmony and tenderness which has
subsisted between you and your young companions I have
hitherto regarded with equal approbation and pleasure;
but the season now approaches when, even by the excess
of a laudable and virtuous sensibility, you may be betrayed
into a situation the most threatening and perilous. You
are now no longer children; you are too lovely and too
susceptible to indulge in an intercourse, however amiable,
innocent, and full of charms, which may lead to consequences that timely caution only can avert. Were it not
for certain prejudices, which the world has agreed to respect and to observe, I should perceive your growing tenderness with delight, and hail it as the presage and the
security of virtue; but I am responsible to another tribunal
than that of *reason* and my own heart for the sentiments
and conduct of this young man, and I dare not betray my
trust. Your childish association has been a reciprocal
source of moral and mental improvement: thus far let us
congratulate ourselves, and reap the benefit: but the imperious usages of society, with a stern voice, now command us to pause. Her mandates, often irrational, are,
nevertheless, always despotic: contemn them, — the hazard
is certain, and the penalty may be tremendous. Some vigorous minds dare to encounter these perils: doubtless, we
are indebted to them: they help to shake the fantastic

fabric: but woe be to those who, in this arduous contest, miscalculate their powers! I confess, I wish not to see the name of my girl enrolled in the tragic list either of martyrs or of victims: solicitous for her *happiness*, I would have prudence temper her heroism. Need I enlarge? Must I add — *You can never be the wife of William Pelham?*"

A shock of electricity appeared to rend my quivering nerves; my colour changed, my bosom palpitated, a faint sickness seemed for an instant to stop the current of my blood; the next moment it rushed impetuously through my veins, distended my heart, and dyed my face and neck with crimson. After a short pause, he proceeded.

"His father has far other views for him; views, in which, at a future period, he will probably acquiesce. Yes, the guileless, generous, ardent, youth, brought up in rural shades, on his entrance into society, will, by irresistible contagion and insensible gradations, become a *man of the world*.²² 'Let him be preserved from humiliating connections,' said Mr. Pelham, when he entrusted him to my charge. In the opinion of those who class with the higher ranks of society, poverty, obscure birth, and the want of splendid connections, are the only circumstances by which he can be degraded. The beauty, the virtue, the talents, of my child, in the eye of philosophy, are an invaluable dowry; but philosophers are not yet the legislators of mankind. William is destined for the theatre of the world; he will imbibe the contagion of a distempered civilization. *Mary must not be contemned by the man she loves.*"

My friend ceased to speak, while he pressed my hands in his, and, bending fondly over me, watched every turn of my varying countenance. His impressive manner, the interesting subject of his discourse, had commanded all my attention: a flood of ideas gushed upon my mind, novel, affecting, terrible, and bewildered my disordered senses. Accustomed to love William from my childhood, to receive and to return his innocent and lively caresses, I had not inquired into the nature of my sensations, and I now understood them but obscurely.

Mr. Raymond's discourse had conveyed to me no distinct idea, till 'You can never be the wife of William Pelham,' repeated emphatically, sounded in my startled ears, in which it still continued to vibrate. Many of the sentiments and reflections of my patron struck me as at once new, extraordinary, and inconsistent. My ideas were confused, my reasoning powers suspended: undefined apprehensions and suspicions arose in my mind; my principles were unhinged and my passions thrown into disorder. Mr. Raymond perceived the conflict, the contending feelings, which shook my fluctuating spirits.

"Retire, my beloved girl," said he tenderly, "for the night; try to compose yourself, and reflect on what has passed at your leisure. God forbid that I should tyrannize over your heart: to your own judgement I entrust your conduct. Confide in me with frankness; I may advise, but I will use no control. You are wholly free, your actions unwatched and unrestrained: I abide your determination."

I threw myself into his arms; I regarded him, in silence, with a disturbed and mournful air: he folded me to his bosom, led me to the entrance of my chamber, and quitted me precipitately.

Unhappy parent! unhappy tutor! forced into contradictions that distort and belie thy wisest precepts, that undermine and defeat thy most sagacious purposes! — While the practice of the world opposes the principles of the sage, education is a fallacious effort, morals an empty theory, and sentiment a delusive dream.

Chapter VII

I PASSED THE NIGHT in a tempest of contending passions: I sought to arrange my thoughts and tranquillize my feelings in vain. Mr. Raymond's discourse had awakened in my heart new desires and new terrors, to which, till that moment, it had been a stranger. The novelty of my sensations at once surprised and alarmed me: happy in the present and thoughtless of the future, I had neither dreaded danger nor anticipated vicissitude. If nature had yet spoken in my heart, so soft and gentle were her whispers, that her voice had hitherto been unheeded. The caution of my patron appeared to have given a sudden and premature existence to the sentiment against which he sought to arm me. Acquainted with the human mind, of this effect he was but too well aware; yet, in the critical circumstances in which he found himself, he perceived no other alternative; but, while tenderly sympathizing in the pain he conceived himself compelled to inflict, he confided firmly in the principles he had implanted.

Towards morning, exhausted by perturbation, I sunk into slumber, nor awoke till the day was far advanced. The bright beams of the sun, darting through my curtains, restored me to sense and recollection, and, for the first time in my life, I awoke to anguish. Springing from the bed, I dressed in haste, when a trampling of horses' feet under my window attracted my attention. Hastily opening the casement, I discovered several gentlemen on horseback, attended by servants, in the midst of whom were William and Edmund.

The eyes of William were turned anxiously towards my apartment, when, perceiving me, he uttered a shout of joy, and, throwing himself from his horse, flew back to the house. Trembling, though I knew not why, I descended hastily the stairs, and met him on the landing-place.

"I am going," said he, "my dear Mary," catching me in his arms, and tenderly embracing me, "a short tour with some friends of my father's, and propose to be absent some days. So idle were you this morning, that I began to fear I must quit you without saying *farewel!* and taking a parting kiss."

Mr. Raymond approached: my colour changed, my tremor increased; the caresses of William, no longer received and returned with artless joy, dyed my cheeks with scarlet, poured through my veins a subtle poison, and shook my trembling frame. Precipitately disengaging myself from his embraces, a servant at the same instant hastily summoning him to join his party, I returned to my chamber with faultering steps. Unconsciously, I regained the window: William, as he mounted, waved his hand to me, repeating the action with his face as he rode forwards. Straining my sight to look after him, when the winding of the road concealed him from my view, I burst into a flood of tears. "O God!" exclaimed I, clasping my hands passionately, and raising my streaming eyes, "he is gone! I have seen him, perhaps, for the last time! Why must we be torn asunder? Why can *I never be the wife of William Pelham?* What tyranny is this? When reason, virtue, nature, sanctify its emotions,[23] why should the heart be controlled? who will dare control it?" — I wept anew, sobbed audibly, my bosom bursting with grief. For the first time in my life, I was ready to accuse my guardian of injustice and caprice. It was many hours ere I reasoned myself into more composure.

I remained in my chamber during the greater part of the day. My patron satisfied himself with sending up refreshments and kind inquiries, but made no effort either to see or to converse with me.

In the evening, I sought him in the garden, whither he was accustomed, in mild weather, to repair. Perceiving my approach, he advanced towards me with features expressing kindness and sympathy.

"I am prepared," said I, in a firm tone, my face averted, "to conform myself to your commands."

"*Commands*, Mary! I am no tyrant; I am unaccustomed to command."

"Pardon me, sir, I am sensible of your goodness, but I dare not deceive you. When you tell me that the affection I have hitherto delighted to cherish for your pupil is become dangerous and improper; that certain prejudices, with the nature of which I am unacquainted, rend us asunder, and convert what was innocent and laudable into I know not what of pernicious and criminal; that tremendous judgements and penalties threaten us, from which there is neither appeal nor escape; I confess I comprehend nothing of all this which you have not deigned to unravel: nevertheless, my confidence in your wisdom and kindness impel me to resign myself to your guidance, and to trust, that time and experience will gradually disentangle my apprehensions, and unfold to me what now appears wholly inexplicable."

"Yes, my child! this, at present, I own, is a subject too subtle for reasoning; *time and experience* only can evince the propriety of my conduct. I should confound with reluctance, by factitious distinctions, the rectitude of your judgement, or blast, by worldly maxims, the ingenuous virtues of your expanding mind. Convinced of your sincerity, and aware of your fortitude, I accept the sacrifice you offer; but, while I task your heart and courage, be assured that, by the truest, the tenderest, sympathy, mine is pervaded."

"Yet do not misconceive me, my father; with my present views and feelings, I dare not engage to love William no longer. I pretend to no heroism, though, aware of my inexperience, I yield, for the present, my conduct to your directions. Mark out for me the path I should pursue; my heart assures me that you have not exacted from me this first instance of *implicit resignation* without important reasons, reasons that you will not always think it just to withhold."

Mr. Raymond appeared greatly affected, and sighed deeply. "Mary," said he, in a solemn and plaintive accent, "you have fulfilled my expectations, you have smoothed the difficulty of instruction; a difficulty, alas! of which I have been but too well aware. Human life has not unaptly been compared to a warfare: whether rendered so by nature or by civil institution, it is for future experiments to determine: for the present, we have too frequently but a choice of evils; in which case, to select the lightest is all that benevolence can advise or wisdom perform. What was in my power, the pleasures of childhood, I have laboured to secure to you unalloyed. In a wild and uncertain calculation of the future, the happiness of the *present* (all that properly can be termed our own) ought not to be trifled with: yet there are limits, even upon this principle, that to overleap would become insanity; the present crisis, if I mistake not, marks the boundary, and imperiously calls upon me to dispense with the rule to which I have hitherto sacredly adhered, — That of imposing no penalty on a being capable of reason, without strictly defining the motives by which I am actuated."

"It is enough, sir; tell me where and to whom I shall go; I consent to be banished from all that gives to life its charm; I confide, without shrinking, in your judgement and affection."

"I have a friend," resumed Mr. Raymond, after a pause, "a respectable and worthy man, who resides on the sea-coast, about fifty miles from hence, on a curacy of sixty pounds a year.[24] He is a man of sense and letters, his wife an accomplished amiable woman. By contracting their wants, they contrive to be happy and independent on a scanty stipend. My girl, during the period which I think it necessary to deprive myself of her society, will, I have no doubt, find, under the humble roof of this excellent pair, a cordial welcome and a hospitable asylum. In the bosom of virtue and domestic peace, her mind will quickly regain its wonted serenity. Contemplating the artless picture of nature in one of her rarest and most favoured lots, her heart will expand in delightful sympathy, and, in the simple joys which surround her, quickly lose sight of those overweening considerations which, at present, so entirely absorb it."

"Let us go, my father," seizing his hand, and speaking rapidly, "let us go this moment, ere new trials, before which my strength may melt away, incapacitate me for fulfilling the arduous duties which my misgiving heart already but too forcibly forebodes."

"I understand you, my child, and I respect your resolution; yet forget not that, amidst the vicissitudes and the calamities of life, a firm and an independent mind is an invaluable treasure and a never-failing support. The canker most pernicious to every virtue is *dependence*; and the most fatal species of bondage is subjection to the demands of our own imperious passions.[25] Retire, and court the repose of which your pale cheek and languid eyes but too plainly indicate your need, and to-morrow early we will prepare for the execution of our project."

My dear benefactor embracing me tenderly, I returned to my chamber. To the conflict which had lately shaken my soul, a gloomy tranquillity succeeded; the still whispers of a self-approving heart sustained me; while resting with grateful love and implicit truth, as on omnipotent truth and goodness, in the cares and tenderness of my friend, hope undefined and indistinct consolation stole upon my spirits, and gradually lulled them in balmy repose.

Chapter VIII

I AROSE WITH THE DAWN, and busied myself in preparations for my departure, repelling, with solicitude, every recollection that might enfeeble my spirits or unnerve my resolution. I repeated to myself incessantly, "Has not my kind
patron just and irresistible claims upon the mind which,
with unremitting assiduity, he has laboured to form? Dare
I disappoint his hopes and disgrace his precepts in the moment of trial, the moment which decides the success of his
cares? Have I not, in the whole of his past conduct, at once
considerate, wise, and good, a foundation for my trust?
Does he sternly call upon me to submit to authority? Is it
to his own passions he requires the sacrifice of mine? Does
he assume the vindictive tone of an infallible judge, from
whose decisions there remains no appeal? Does he, with
stoic pride, insult the sensibilities for which nature has incapacitated his heart, or which time and experience have
combined to chill? Does he mock the feelings, does he contemn the weakness, which his firmer mind repels? Ah, no!
it is not the austere parent, the tutor, the patron, who, presuming on his claims, derides the tenderness and the ardour of youth; no, it is the friend, gentle, candid, benignant,
contemning every privilege, disdaining all subterfuge, using
no deception, who, while constrained to wound the heart
through which he has been wont to diffuse gladness, weeps
in tender sympathy; who, while he confesses reserve, and laments its necessity, appeals to the rectitude of his past conduct, appeals to the kindness to which every action, every
expression, every feature, bear irresistible testimony. Nor
shall he appeal in vain: a confidence thus generous I dare
not betray. Far be from my heart, then, these weak and
womanish regrets: to a determined spirit, to suffer is not

difficult; but the vice of ingratitude shall never taint my soul."

A generous heroism nerved my mind, throbbed in my bosom, glowed on my cheek, a spirit congenial to artless youth, by whom the veil of society, behind which corruption and contradiction lurk, has not been rent. My eyes regained their lustre, and my features their wonted spirit.

On the first summons, I joined Mr. Raymond at the breakfast-table: he read, in the serenity, the triumph, of my countenance, the victory I had gained. How sweet, how grateful, were his approving smiles! I enjoyed them as an earnest of future conquests, as a reward to which my heart proudly whispered its claim.

A chaise[26] drew up to the door, into which, followed by my benefactor, I lightly sprang. Stifling a sigh, and seizing the reins, I quickly left behind the scene of all my pleasures, while peace spread its halcyon[27] wings, and fled for ever.

Every subsequent incident of an eventful life has but led the way to new persecutions and new sorrows, against which the purest intentions, the most unconquerable fortitude, the most spotless innocence, have availed me nothing. Entangled in a series of unavoidable circumstances, hemmed in by insuperable obstacles, overwhelmed by a torrent of resistless prejudice, wearied with opposition, and exhausted by conflict, I yield, at length, to a destiny against which precautions and struggles have been alike fruitless.

Chapter IX

IT WAS LATE IN THE EVENING when we drew near the place of our destination. Alighting at a small neat house, in the cottage-style, with barns and out-houses adjoining, we were met, on our entrance, by its respectable owner, who, on recognizing Mr. Raymond, uttered an exclamation of mingled joy and surprise.

"To what fortunate accident," said he, in a tone of animation, cordially greeting his friend, "am I indebted for this unexpected pleasure?"

"I have a charge," replied my guardian, "a precious charge, which, for a short period, I would willingly consign to the protection of my worthy friends, because there is none in whom I have equal confidence."

As he ceased speaking, we entered, conducted by our host, a small parlour, in the simple furniture of which, and ornamental drawings uniformly arranged against an oaken wainscot, an air of taste was manifest. Mrs. Neville, the wife of the curate, was seated near a casement,[28] shaded, on the outside, by the luxuriant foliage of a spreading vine, through which the twilight dimly gleamed. Two children, blooming as cherubs, played at her feet: she held a book in her hand half-closed, over which she seemed to muse. On our entrance, starting from her position, and throwing aside the author who had engaged her attention, she advanced hastily towards us, testifying, on the appearance of Mr. Raymond, a lively joy. Some minutes past in mutual inquiries and congratulations.

"Behold," said my benefactor, taking my hand, and presenting me to his friends, "behold the dear child in whose praises my heart has so often overflowed with all a parent's partial fondness! I am constrained, for a time, to bereave myself of her presence: do I presume too far on your friendship when I flatter myself that, beneath your hospitable roof, I may, for a while, secure to her a welcome asylum?"

With a conciliating grace, this amiable pair frankly accepted the proffered trust, quickly re-assuring, by a polished urbanity of manners, my doubting spirits. Lights being brought and refreshments set before us by a rustic maiden, past times and occurrences became the subjects of conversation in this little circle of friends, during which I had leisure to contemplate more minutely the manners and lineaments of my hosts. Mr. Neville appeared to be between five-and-thirty and forty years of age: his figure was tall and commanding, his complexion florid: dark brown hair unsoiled by powder,[29] and parting on his forehead, contrasted its whiteness: his aspect was somewhat severe, bold, and manly, yet tempered by benignity, repelling assumption rather than inspiring dread: his manners were cheerful, his temper apparently equal, his conversation intelligent, bespeaking a mind alike conversant with men and books: his sentiments occasionally assumed a higher tone, discovering a latent ardour and an activity of mind for which his present situation afforded insufficient scope; but a momentary recollection seemed to check these feelings, and restore to his temper its habitual serenity. The appearance of Mrs. Neville, who was somewhat younger than her husband, indicated a delicacy of original texture rather than an infirm state of health. Her complexion was olive, inclining to pale, yet varying with exercise or sentiment, when a charming flush would crimson her cheek: her eyes were dark, mild, and penetrating, yet susceptible of spirit when kindled by passion or sentiment: her countenance, without pretension to beauty, had in it an expression full of sense and soul: there was a fascination in her smile; and her flexible voice, when modulated by tenderness, took the affections captive: an emphatic propriety marked her pronunciation, her mind seemed stored with knowledge, though of a varied and desultory nature, her imagination elevated, and not wholly untinctured with romantic views and feelings: her manners were habitually serious, an excessive sensibility at times even gave them the appearance of melancholy, but, exquisitely sensible to social pleasure, in the presence of those whom her heart acknowledged, she became animated and sprightly: the predominant passion of her soul, testified in every action, every expression, every glance, was, an enthusiastic love for her husband, a love at once ineffably tender, chaste, and dignified: her children were little less the objects of her tender solicitude.

It was not possible for a heart like mine to contemplate this interesting family without a lively prepossession: I anticipated the pleasure of cultivating their friendship and expanding my sensations. Involuntarily I repeated to myself, "Why cannot I, with sweet magic, draw into one circle all I revere and love? Why cannot I increase and multiply, a million-fold, these delightful sympathies? — My heart, with inexpressible yearnings, continually prompts me to unite, to bind, myself to my fellow-beings by every social and relative tie."

On retiring for the night, I was conducted by Mrs. Neville to a small neat chamber, where, after renewing her assurances of a friendly welcome, and kindly soothing my agitated spirits, she left me to my repose. Mr. Raymond, having resisted the solicitations of his friends for a longer residence under their hospitable roof, had signified his intention of departing early in the ensuing morning. I rose with the sun, and hastened to his apartment. My dear benefactor, little less affected than myself by our first mournful separation, folded me to his bosom, and, while I wept in his arms, mingled his tears with mine.

"Your tenderness, my sweet girl," said he, "pierces my heart; your sensibility unmans me. I have, perhaps, been wrong: God knows, I would not inflict on your gentle nature one unnecessary pang: even now, if you request it, you shall return with me. I impose no fetters, I will trust to the rectitude of your feelings."

"No, my friend, my father," replied I, in a voice half-stifled with emotion: "forgive my weakness: my confidence in you is unbounded, but nature will, for a time, assert her powerful rights. You have just claims upon my fortitude, upon my affection. Go! leave me! You will not, you cannot, forget your child!"

I struggled with my feelings, and suppressed my tears. I dared not pronounce the name of *William*, a name engraven on my heart, a name for ever on my lips. My patron read in my eyes the law which I imposed on myself: he pressed my hand, sighed, averted his face. Once more tenderly embracing me, he precipitately quitted the room, accompanied by our host, who, entering at the same instant, had invited him to partake of a refreshment prepared by Mrs. Neville, and informed him that the chaise was in readiness.

I returned to my chamber, where I remained till summoned to the breakfast-table. I had, during the interval, reasoned myself into more composure, and, rejoining my friends with assumed cheerfulness, sought to banish from my heart every enervating remembrance, every despondent feeling.

In a few days, my mind appeared to have recovered, as with an elastic force, from the sudden shock it had sustained, and to have resumed its habitual cheerfulness. I sought occupation, and assisted Mrs. Neville in her domestic economy and in the management of her diary. By admirable order, attention, and dexterity, this amiable pair, upon an annual income of sixty pounds,[30] contrived to preserve even an air of liberality. It is true, the product of a well-planted garden, and the profits of a few acres of land, cultivated by the labour of the worthy curate,[31] added something to their yearly store. The morning, lengthened by early rising, was devoted to business, in which equal skill and perseverance were displayed. In the after-part of the day, literature, music, the instruction of their children, a ramble among the neighbouring hamlets, (to the sick and infirm inhabitants of which they were beneficent friends,) a walk on the sea-beach, through the meadows, or on the downs, divided their time. Not an hour passed unimproved or vacant: when confined by inclement seasons to their tranquil home, Mrs. Neville employed herself with her needle in preparing simple vestments for her household, while her husband read aloud selected passages from a small collection of books, which was annually increased by an appropriated sum. Music frequently concluded the evening: Mrs. Neville touched the piano-forte with more feeling than skill, and accompanied by her voice (sweet, but without compass) simple canzonets, impassioned airs, or plaintive ballads.

Through this happy family, perfect harmony and tenderness reigned: Mr. Neville loved and entirely confided in his wife, of whose value he was justly sensible; while her affection for him had in it I know not what of tender solicitude, of exquisite softness, of ardent devotion, which, to hearts less susceptible, would appear excessive or inconceivable. Their children, lovely and promising, were equally their delight and care: they formed, between their parents, a new and a more sacred bond: their expanding faculties and budding graces authorized and justified a parent's fondest hopes. *Happiness*, coy and fair fugitive, who shunnest the gaudy pageants of courts and cities, the crowded haunts of vanity, the rootless cares of ambition, the insatiable pursuits of avarice, the revels of voluptuousness, and the riot of giddy mirth, who turneth alike from fastidious refinement and brutal ignorance, if, indeed, thou art not a phantom that mockest our research, thou art only to be found in the real solid pleasures of nature and social affection.

Chapter X

IN THE BOSOM OF THIS charming retirement, several weeks glided away in tranquillity. I received frequent letters from my guardian, which spoke of his pupils, but in general terms. The health of Edmund, he informed me, appeared to decline daily: a warmer climate had been advised by his physicians, in consequence of which, Mr. Pelham appeared inclined to send his sons on a continental tour, but that nothing was yet determined upon.

A train of painful reflections revived in my mind on this intelligence: how could I daily behold the tender and rational felicity of the interesting family in which I resided, and preserve my heart from drawing painful comparisons? How could I suppress secret murmurs at the factitious scruples to which I seemed a victim? Torn from my lover, he had, perhaps, disgusted with my inexplicable conduct, resigned and forgotten me. He wrote not, he came not: "Already," I sighed to myself, "he is become *a man of the world!* He doubtless acquiesces, without reluctance, in those senseless prejudices to which I have tamely submitted, whose nature I am utterly unable to comprehend." My mind became disquieted, my spirits lost their tone, disgust seized upon me, my wonted amusements were tasteless, I avoided the society of my friends, their mutual endearments pierced my soul, and filled my eyes with tears. I sought solitude, and sunk into gloomy rêveries.

Wandering one evening alone upon the beach, I seated myself on a jutting part of a rock, overhanging the sea: the air was serene, the breeze sighed softly, the waves, slowly succeeding each other, broke on the shore, and the surf dashed at my feet: every object was in unison with my feelings. As I contemplated the expanse of the waters which flowed around me, a mournful solemnity stole over my spirits: absorbed in thought, the tide, which was rising, insensibly gained upon me, and it was not till my retreat was cut off that I observed myself encompassed by the waves, and became conscious to the perils of my situation. — My feet were already wet, and the spray of the sea dashed over me. I started with an involuntary emotion of terror, and, casting my eyes around for succour, thought I perceived at a distance, through the obscurity of the twilight, an object white, but indistinct, which, on its nearer approach, I discovered with joy to be a sail. I waved my handkerchief, as a signal of distress, and uttered a loud cry. The boat at length drew near, appearing to contain a party of gentlemen, who hailed me as it advanced. I continued to wave my handkerchief, and, in a few minutes, was extricated from my danger, and lifted by one of the gentlemen into the vessel.

"By G-d, my pretty maid," said my deliverer, observing my garments wet, "you were in a critical situation, and have had a fortunate escape."

A shuddering seized me on recognizing the voice of Sir Peter Osborne. Since the adventure of the chase, I had seen him occasionally pass the house of Mr. Raymond, to whom he had made some overtures towards an acquaintance, which my patron had uniformly evaded. I had once or twice met him in my rambles, but had always fled from him, and, till this moment, had avoided a direct recontre. I drew my hat over my face, and, shrinking from his bold eyes, accepted, without reply, a seat which was offered me. My silence being imputed to the effects of my late apprehensions, the gentlemen pressed me to take refreshment, which, bowing, I rejected with a motion of my hand. The odious Osborne, who appeared to be inebriated, was not to be thus repulsed: seating himself beside me, and peering under my hat, he encircled my waist with his left arm, while, with his right hand, he seized mine. Struggling to disengage myself,

"I presume, gentlemen," said I, with spirit, "you do not conceive yourselves entitled, by the relief you have accidentally afforded me, a relief which gives me a double claim upon your honour and humanity, to treat me with insult."

"Faith!" exclaimed my persecutor, "it is so; I suspected it from the very first glance; it is my fair fugitive herself."

"Yes, sir," replied I, with increased vivacity, "I am, indeed, the young woman who has been, more than once, a sufferer from your brutality. I insist upon being released this moment. I do not expect from you the manners of a gentleman, but I will not be intimidated or constrained."

The wretch seemed struck with a temporary awe by my resolute and spirited manner. His companions interfering, he was persuaded, though not without imprecations and reluctance, to relinquish his seat.

We landed in safety, and, escorted by the whole party, who would not be prevailed upon to leave me, I repaired to the cottage of my friends. Mr. Neville, having been alarmed by my unusual absence and the lateness of the hour, had but just returned from an anxious and fruitless search. I was welcomed by my amiable hosts with unaffected joy, when my conductors, having received polite and fervent acknowledgements for their timely interposition, departed.

Early in the ensuing morning, a servant, in a gay livery,[32] arrived, with a billet of inquiry, from Sir Peter, after my rest and health; to which was added an apology for his behaviour of the preceding evening, and an entreaty to be allowed to pay his respects to me. To this epistle I returned a brief and cold answer, thanking him for the service he had been instrumental in rendering me, and declining the proposed visit.

In the vicinity of the village in which I at present resided, was a town of fashionable resort, for the benefit of sea-bathing; the season for which being now at its height, sufficiently accounted for the late incident.

My repulses served but to stimulate my tormentor: he beset my paths, haunted me daily, and overwhelmed me with adulation and offensive gallantry. His understanding, though not of the highest order, was by no means contemptible, but his manners were profligate and presuming; they alike provoked my indignation and disgust. I at length determined, during his stay in the country, to confine myself wholly to the house: but neither did this avail me; he forced himself upon Mr. Neville with an undaunted effrontery, breaking in upon our employments and recreations, till my friend, justly incensed, resolved to submit no longer to an intrusion thus unseasonable and impertinent. Upon his next visit, he signified to him in firm, but temperate, language, that his company was unwelcome, that it was an interruption to the occupations of the family, that it was offensive to his guest, and that he must beg leave, in future, to decline an acquaintance equally unwished-for and unsuitable.

This plain and manly remonstrance, though impatiently received and haughtily resented, nevertheless produced its effect: yet, on quitting the house, the insolent man of fashion menaced my host, in obscure terms, with future retribution. Tender fears were, by this incident, awakened in the breast of Mrs. Neville for the safety of her beloved husband; but, in a few days, to our mutual relief, we were informed that our adversary had actually quitted that part of the country.

Chapter XI

SOME WEEKS AFTER these transactions, my friends being from home, on a visit of humanity, sitting one evening alone in my apartment, indulging in a melancholy retrospect, I was roused from my rêverie by the entrance of the servant-girl, who hastily informed me that a fine young gentleman, (a stranger,) on horseback, had that moment arrived; that, having alighted and inquired for Miss Raymond, she had conducted him into the parlour, where he waited with seeming impatience to speak to me. I changed colour; a flattering conjecture darted through my mind, while an universal tremor seized my limbs. With a throbbing heart and faultering steps, I repaired to the parlour, and, the next instant, found myself in the arms of William. It was some time before either of us acquired sufficient composure for articulate expression; our joy was excessive and tumultuous; we mingled tears with our mutual embraces. My lover overwhelmed me with broken and tender reproaches for having quitted him so abruptly, for having so long left him uncertain of my situation.

"Alas!" replied I, "did you know what I have suffered —" I hesitated: my heart was rent by contending passions; confused notions of danger and impropriety, of respect for the judgement of my guardian, struggled with my native sincerity: I trembled; I felt the blood alternately forsake and rush back to my heart, which a faint sickness overspread. I sunk into a chair, and remained silent.

"I understand you," said William, regarding me with a passionate and mournful air, "but too well: you are a victim to control, you have tamely submitted to a tyranny that your heart disavows; your wonted spirit and firmness are subdued."

"Hold!" resumed I, "be not unjust! Mr. Raymond, in

the sacrifice which he requires of us, is guided by considerations the most disinterested: he imposes nothing, he
appeals to my reason and affections, and his claims are
resistless. I understand not, I confess, the extent of the
motives which influence him; but assuredly his past conduct entitles him to my trust." — I proceeded to relate
what had passed between my patron and myself previous
to our departure. — "I knew not," added I, in a low accent,
with downcast eyes and an averted face, "that the regard
I felt for you differed, in any respect, from our mutual
and infantine fondness, till Mr. Raymond awakened my
fears, and alarmed my tenderness, by telling me that I
must separate myself from you, that 'I must never be the
wife of William Pelham,' that he would become *a man of
the world*, and contemn my artless affection."

"It is false," replied William with vehemence, who had
listened to my recital with evident indignation and impatience, "it is false as hell! *I love you*, Mary, and will never
receive any other wife. Mr. Raymond does my father injustice: it is true, he is the slave of honour, but he is not
sordid: an alliance with your guardian, a man of education
and a gentleman, to whom, no doubt, you are connected
by ties of blood, will do our family no discredit, and *love*
will make us happy, though our fortunes should be moderate."

My lover proceeded to paint his passion with all the
eloquence of ardent, youthful, feeling. He informed me,
that, after my departure, he had sunk into sadness; that
he knew not, till then, the excess of his affection for me;
that his tutor had, for some time, evaded his inquiries,
but, at length, overcome by his importunity, had named
to him the place of my present abode, at the same time
recapitulating and enforcing the motives of his conduct.
"Immediately," added he, "I procured a horse, and, with-

out speaking of my intentions, early the next morning took the road to this place, where I have but now arrived."

The return of Mr. and Mrs. Neville, to whom I introduced my friend as a pupil of Mr. Raymond, put a period to our discourse. They pressed him, during his stay in the country, to accept an apartment at their house, a request to which he acceded with visible satisfaction. Racking inquietude disturbed my mind, as various passions bewildered my judgement and assailed my heart. I discerned not on which side lay the path of duty: my reason became weakened by contradictory principles. Thus, the moment the dictates of virtue, direct and simple, are perplexed by false scruples and artificial distinctions, the mind becomes entangled in an inextricable labyrinth, to which there is no clue, and whence there is no escape.

I threw myself on my bed, at the hour of retirement, vainly seeking to collect and arrange my scattered thoughts: sleep fled from my eye-lids; I arose, and, seizing a pen, addressed my benefactor.

I acquainted him with the arrival of his pupil; I endeavoured to paint to him my emotions; I besought his aid; I expostulated with him respecting the task he had imposed upon me; I reproached him for the conflict to which he had exposed me; I regretted the placid days of my childhood; and confessed I understood but obscurely the causes of the change which I experienced. − "I am not weak," said I, "neither will I be the slave of my passions. *I love William Pelham*, but am ready to renounce him the moment my reason is convinced that virtue demands the sacrifice."

Having thus poured out my spirit, I became more tranquil. A few hours slumber refreshed my wearied faculties, yet the morning found me dejected and languid.

William, charmed with the interesting manners and

family of his hosts, spoke with rapture of their mutual tenderness. "How poor, how contemptible," said he, "are fortune's most lavish gifts! Why, my sweet girl, should we suffer the prejudices of others to enslave us? Let us purchase a cottage, and hide ourselves from the world, supremely blest in each other. What can be added to the felicity of mutual love?"

I sighed involuntarily. "Yes, my friend, I doubt not that such are your present feelings. While my own heart beats with responsive sympathies, I know not why I should distrust their continuance; yet how can I efface from that misgiving heart the fearful presage that even yet vibrates on my startled ear, — 'Mary will be contemned by the man she loves; William Pelham will become *a man of the world.*'?"

"Cruel and unjust girl! how have I merited suspicions thus injurious?"

Ah! how full of charms, how insidious, is the eloquence of a beloved object! While my lover pictured to my imagination, in glowing colours, the pleasures of an union which nature, reason, and virtue,[33] should combine to render perfect, my heart melted within me, I caught the ineffable sympathy, the injunctions of my patron faded from before me, I became animated, as it were, with new powers, with a new existence, time seemed doubled by a lively and exquisite consciousness to every instant as it passed; yet, undefinable contradiction! I regretted its rapid flight, and panted to eternize the fleeting moments. — "We loved each other; we beheld only our mutual perfections: in the midst of our transports, we mingled our tears, tears purer than the dew of heaven; delicious tears, creating the most exquisite rapture. We were in that be witching delirium which rendered even the constraint we imposed upon ourselves an honourable sacrifice that added a zest to our happiness."*[34]

* Rousseau *Emille* [Hays' note]

Chapter XII

FROM THESE ENCHANTING VISIONS I was at length roused
by a packet from my guardian. Retiring to my apartment, I
unfolded it with emotion.

"My child," said this revered friend, "your present circumstances wring from my heart a narrative that will
wound your gentle nature; a narrative which it was my
purpose for ever to have withheld from you. I yield, with
anguish, to the necessity and to the perils of your situation.

"You have hitherto remained ignorant of the authors
of your birth; I studied to supply to you paternal duties;
it was my care that nothing should remind you of their
loss. I succeeded: all your hours were marked with active
enjoyment. I cultivated your faculties and exercised your
affections: I left you no time for languor or retrospect.
Aware of the disadvantages which might, too probably,
attend your progress in life, I sought what was in my
power, to secure to you without alloy the happiness of
the present: yet it was my arduous purpose, while promoting your enjoyment, to render even your pleasures sub-
servient to a higher view, — That of invigorating your
frame and fortifying your spirit, that you might be prepared to meet the future, to suffer its trials, and brave its
vicissitudes, with courage and dignity. I perceive, with self-
gratulation, the fruit of my labours; I see in you all that
my most sanguine wishes presaged. I know you equal to
encounter, to be victorious, in the conflict that awaits you;
a conflict in which my affection and prudence can no
longer avail you. But, while anticipating your victory, believe me not unmindful of your sufferings: while I perceive
in them the seeds of future strength and energy, my cow-

ard heart and fostering arms yearn to shelter the child of my bosom from the gathering storm. I proceed to state to you those particulars of your birth, which, in your present circumstances, become too important to justify a longer concealment.

"The younger brother of a respectable family, at the age of one-and-twenty, with a liberal education and a small fortune, I became master of myself and of my actions. I passed some years in the dissipations customary to young men of my age and rank: at length, wearied with a heartless intercourse, while my fortune daily diminished, I determined to seek, from the interest of my numerous acquaintance, some lucrative office; to marry, and cultivate domestic endearments. In these dispositions, I saw, and became enamoured of, a young woman, amiable and accomplished, the idol of fond, but weak, parents, who had lavished, on the adornment of this darling, for whose advancement they had formed ambitious projects, sums which their fortunes were little able to sustain. I frankly, though somewhat indiscreetly, offered to the lovely Mary, whom Nature had formed in her most perfect mould, my hand and my heart. Rejecting my address with expressions of respect, she ingenuously acknowledged that her heart had already surrendered itself; yet, with an engaging air, she solicited my friendship; modestly adding that, affected by the promptitude and generosity of my proposals, it would be her pride to be deemed worthy of my esteem.

"I continued occasionally to see her: I watched in vain for my rival, with the jealous eye of love: an air of mystery seemed to hang over the affair, which I was utterly unable to penetrate. My fair friend became restless and disquieted; languor overspread her fine features, internal agitation preyed upon her spirits, her temper grew unequal, her bloom faded, and her health appeared daily to decline. I perceived the struggles of her mind; I perceived that a secret malady devoured her: I sought her confidence, with a determination of serving her, to the sacrifice of my own feelings; but all my inquiries were uniformly evaded. Finding our intercourse useless to her, and destructive of my own peace, I began to meditate its dissolution. An offer occurred of accompanying a young man, a college-friend, on a foreign tour. Eagerly availing myself of this opportunity, I agreed to an immediate departure, expecting that change of objects, time, and absence, would produce on my mind their usual effects.

"At the expiration of five years, I returned to my native land: a series of dissipation had almost effaced from my heart the traces of its former impressions, till they were painfully renewed by a catastrophe full of horror. Returning, one evening, at a late hour, with a party of friends, from a convivial meeting, our ears were assailed, as we passed a tavern of doubtful reputation, with a tumultuous noise, in which, amidst shouts and imprecations, the shrieks of women and the cries of murder, mingled with the clashing of swords, might plainly be distinguished. Rushing towards the apartment from whence the alarm appeared to proceed, we perceived, amidst a promiscuous group of people, a gentleman extended on the floor, bathed in blood, who appeared to be expiring. Beside him stood a man, with a fierce and gloomy aspect, forcibly detained by the spectators, from whom he struggled to free himself. A woman, with a wan and haggard countenance, her clothes rent and her hair dishevelled, had fainted in the arms of a ruffian who supported her.

"'Secure them,' exclaimed the master of the hotel, to a constable who entered with the watch; 'those are the murderers!'

"It was some time before we could learn the particulars of the terrible scene that presented itself to us, which, we were at length informed, had originated in a brutal and licentious contention for the favours of the unhappy wretch who had fainted, and who was accused of holding, while his antagonist stabbed him, the arm of the dying man.

"In the midst of the tumult, my eyes involuntarily returned every moment to the features of the miserable cause of this catastrophe: the remains of uncommon beauty might still be traced in a form and countenance stained with blood, disordered by recent inebriation, disfigured by vice, and worn by disease. A confused recollection bewildered my thoughts, and gave to my heart a quicker impulse. As, absorbed in reflection, I continued to gaze upon her, she breathed a heavy sigh, and, raising her languid eye-lids, her eyes, wild and vacant, encountered mine: by degrees, their expression became more fixed and recollected; she appeared eagerly to examine my features; a flush overspread her livid countenance, succeeded by a death-like paleness. Starting from the arms of the person who supported her, and clasping her hands with convulsive energy, in a tone piercing and tremulous, she pronounced my name, and, uttering a deep groan, fell in a fit at my feet. The sound of her voice thrilled through my soul; my ideas succeeded to each other with the rapidity of lightning, while my heart instantly recognized, in a situation thus tremendous and degrading, the idol of its youthful affections, the lovely, unfortunate, self abandoned, Mary! — Great God! what, in that terrible moment, were my emotions! — The blood poured in a tide towards my brain, hollow sounds rang in my ears, the lights danced before my dazzled sight, every object became indistinct: I staggered some paces backward, while palpable darkness appeared to envelope me. — Returning to recollection, I gazed around me in vain for the phantom which seemed to have unsettled my reason. The room was cleared, a waiter and one of my companions only remaining: these were chafing my hands and temples with vinegar, and assiduously busying themselves in promoting my recovery.

"In reply to my incoherent and frantic inquiries, I learned that the wounded man had expired, the weapon, on examination, being found to have penetrated his lungs; that the murderer, with the wretched woman his accomplice, had been conveyed to prison, the latter apparently insensible.

"On the succeeding morning, in a state of inconceivable anguish, I repaired to the gaol. I knew not how to inquire for the wretched victim of sensuality and vice by a name enthusiastically treasured in my memory; a name associated with every tender, every melting, recollection; a name held by my imagination sacred and unsullied; a name, which, till the last fatal evening, to pronounce without reverence I should have considered as profanation! I started and shuddered as the gaoler abruptly sounded it in my ears. I put into his hand a piece of gold, in return for which he brought me a slip of paper, blotted and scarcely legible, in which, with great difficulty, I deciphered the following words: —

"'*To* MR. RAYMOND.

"'I knew you; and, by my emotion, betrayed myself to you. There wanted but this to fill up the measure of my shame. I am about to expiate my crimes: seek not to avert my fate. In surviving virtue and fame, I have already lived but too long. I yearn for death: should I find it not in the justice of my country, my own arm shall effect my deliverance. I owe to you a history of my disgrace: expect it, if my heart-strings burst not previously asunder. My dying-request will accompany the infamous tale. In the mean time, make no effort to see me — unless the man, whose invaluable heart I once contemned, seeks to glut his vengeance by beholding me expire at his feet! — Return! Disturb not my remnant of life! We meet no more!

"'MARY.'

"I regained my apartments: a gush of tears relieved my boiling brain; I wept with infantine tenderness. Secluding myself from society, I waited, in dreadful suspense, the issue of these cruel transactions.

"Some weeks elapsed. The trial of the unhappy culprit drew near. Considering her prohibition as the querulous language of despair, I strained every nerve, I left no effort untried, to soften the evidence of her guilt, to avert or to mitigate her sentence. My endeavours were fruitless: condemnation was pronounced, and received with triumph rather than with submission. I sought to procure a parting-interview: my solicitations were uniformly and steadily rejected. The fatal morning now arrived when the woman on whom my soul had once fondly doated, whom yet, in her fallen state, my heart yearned to snatch from the cruel destiny which awaited her, forfeited her life on a scaffold, by the hands of the executioner, to the sanguinary and avenging laws of her country.

"My child! I would have spared both you and myself this terrible recital. The wounds of my heart, thus rudely torn open, bleed afresh. I hasten, from the soul-sickening recollection, to the development of what yet nearer imports you. Read, in the enclosed packet, the memorial conveyed to my hand the day subsequent to this deplorable catastrophe.

"'*To* MR. RAYMOND.

"'How far shall I go back? From what period shall I

date the source of those calamities which have, at length, overwhelmed me? — Educated in the lap of indolence, enervated by pernicious indulgence, fostered in artificial refinements, misled by specious, but false, expectations, softened into imbecility, pampered in luxury, and dazzled by a frivolous ambition, at the age of eighteen, I rejected the manly address and honest ardour of the man whose reason would have enlightened, whose affection would have supported me; through whom I might have enjoyed the endearing relations, and fulfilled the respectable duties, of mistress, wife, and mother; and listened to the insidious flatteries of a being, raised by fashion and fortune to a rank seducing to my vain imagination, in the splendour of which my weak judgement was dazzled and my virtue overpowered.

"'He spoke of tenderness and honour, (prostituted names!) while his actions gave the lie to his pretentions. He affected concealment, and imposed on my understanding by sophistical pretences.[35] Unaccustomed to reason, too weak for principle, credulous from inexperience, a stranger to the corrupt habits of society, I yielded to the mingled intoxication of my vanity and my senses, quitted the paternal roof, and resigned myself to my triumphant seducer.

"'Months revolved in a round of varied pleasures: reflection was stunned in the giddy whirl. I awoke not from my delirium, till, on an unfounded, affected, pretence of jealousy, under which satiety veiled itself, I found myself suddenly deserted, driven with opprobrium from the house of my *destroyer*, thrown friendless and destitute upon the world, branded with infamy, and a wretched outcast from social life. To fill up the measure of my distress, a little time convinced me that I was about to become a mother. The money which remained from my profuse habits was nearly exhausted. In the prospect of immediate distress, I addressed myself to the author of my woes. Relating my situation, I implored his justice and mercy. I sought in vain to awaken his tenderness, to touch his callous heart. To my humble supplications no answer was vouchsafed. Despair, for awhile, with its benumbing power, seized upon my heart!

"'Awakening to new anguish, and recalling my scattered faculties, I remembered the softness and the ease of my childhood, the doating fondness of my weak, but indulgent, parents. I resolved to address them, resolved to pour out before them the confession of my errors, of my griefs, and of my contrition. My lowly solicitations drew upon me bitter reproaches: I was treated as an abandoned wretch, whom it would be criminal to relieve and hopeless to attempt to reclaim.

"'At this crisis, I was sought out and discovered by a friend (if friendship can endure the bond of vice) of my destroyer; the man who, to gratify his sensuality, had entailed, on an unoffending being, *a being who loved him*, misery and certain perdition. My declining virtue, which yet struggled to retrieve itself, was now assailed by affected sympathy, by imprecations on the wretch who had deserted me, and an offer of asylum and protection.

"'My heart, though too weak for principle, was not yet wholly corrupted: the modest habits of female youth were still far from being obliterated; I suspected the views of the guileful deceiver, and contemned them with horror and just indignation. Changing his manners, this Proteus assumed a new form; prophaned the names of humanity, friendship, virtue; gradually inspiring me with confidence. Unable to labour, ashamed to solicit charity, helpless, pennyless, feeble, delicate, thrown out with reproach from society, borne down with a consciousness of irretrievable error, exposed to insult, to want, to contumely, to every species of aggravated distress, in a situation requiring sympathy, tenderness, assistance, — From whence was I to draw fortitude to combat these accumulated evils? By what magical power or supernatural aid was a being, rendered, by all the previous habits of life and education, systematically weak and helpless, at once to assume a courage thus daring and heroic?

"'I received, as the tribute of humanity and friendship, that assistance, without which I had not the means of existence, and was delivered, in due time, of a lovely female infant. While bedewing it with my tears, (delicious tears! tears that shed a balm into my lacerated spirit!) I forgot for awhile its barbarous father, the world's scorn, and my blasted prospects: the sensations of the injured woman, of the insulted wife, were absorbed for a time in the stronger sympathies of the delighted mother.

"'My new friend, to whose tender cares I seemed indebted for the sweet emotions which now engrossed my heart, appeared entitled to my grateful esteem: my confidence in him became every hour more unbounded. It was long ere he stripped off the mask so successfully assumed; when, too late, I found myself betrayed, and became, a second time, the victim of my simplicity and the inhuman arts of a practised deceiver, who had concerted with the companion of his licentious revels, wearied with his conquest, the snare into which I fell a too-credulous prey.

"'Evil communication, habits of voluptuous extravagance, despair of retrieving a blasted fame, gradually stifled the declining struggles of virtue; while the libertine manners of those, of whom I was now compelled to be the associate, rapidly advanced the corruption;

"'Took off the rose
"'From the fair forehead of an innocent love,
"'And plac'd a blister there.[36]

"'In a mind unfortified by principle, modesty is a blossom
fragile as lovely. Every hour, whirled in a giddy round of dissipation, sunk me deeper in shameless vice. The mother became stifled in my heart: my visits to my infant, which I had
been reluctantly prevailed upon to place with a hireling,
were less and less frequent. Its innocence contrasted my
guilt, it revived too powerfully in my heart the remembrance of what I was, the reflection on what I might have
been, and the terrible conviction, which I dared not dwell
upon, of the fate which yet menaced me. I abstained from
this soul-harrowing indulgence, and the ruin of my mind became complete.

"'Why should I dwell upon, why enter into, a disgusting detail of the gradations of thoughtless folly, guilt, and
infamy? Why should I stain the youthful purity of my unfortunate offspring, into whose hands these sheets may
hereafter fall, with the delineation of scenes remembered
with soul-sickening abhorrence? Let it suffice to say, that,
by enlarging the circle of my observation, though in the
bosom of depravity, my understanding became enlightened: I perceived myself the victim of the injustice, of the
prejudice, of society, which, by opposing to my return to
virtue almost insuperable barriers, had plunged me into
irremediable ruin. I grew sullen, desperate, hardened. I
felt a malignant joy in retaliating upon mankind a part of
the evils which I sustained. My mind became fiend-like,
revelling in destruction, glorying in its shame. Abandoned
to excessive and brutal licentiousness, I drowned returning reflection in inebriating potions. The injuries and insults to which my odious profession exposed me eradi-

cated from my heart every remaining human feeling. I
became a monster, cruel, relentless, ferocious; and con-
taminated alike, with a deadly poison, the health and the
principles of those unfortunate victims whom, with practised allurements, I entangled in my snares. Man, however
vicious, however cruel, reaches not the depravity of a
shameless woman. *Despair* shuts not against him every avenue to repentance; *despair* drives him not from human
sympathies; *despair* hurls him not from hope, from pity,
from life's common charities, to plunge him into desperate, damned, guilt.

"'Let the guileful seducer pause here, and tremble!
Let the sordid voluptuary, the thoughtless libertine, stop,
amidst his selfish gratifications, and reflect! Oh! let him
balance this tremendous price, this deplorable ruin,
against the revel of an hour, the revel over which satiety
hovers, and to which disgust and lassitude quickly succeed!
Boast not, vain man, of civil refinements, while, in the
bosom of thy most polished and populous cities, an evil
is fostered, poisoning virtue at its source, diffusing
through every rank its deadly venom, bursting the bonds
of nature, blasting its endearments, destroying the promise of youth, the charm of domestic affections, and hurling
its hapless victims to irremediable perdition.

"'The evening, which completed my career of crime,
roused my slumbering conscience. To *murder* I was yet
unfamiliarized. In the instant when remorse, with its serpent-sting,[37] transfixed my heart, I beheld, with unspeak-
able confusion and anguish, the man who had, with honourable tenderness, sought the chaste affections of my
youth. A thousand poignant emotions rushed upon my
soul: regret, shame, terror, contrition, combined to con-
vulse my enfeebled frame. Through the dead silence of
the night, amidst the prison's gloom, contending passions

rent my tortured spirit: in the bitterness of despair, I dashed my wretched body against the dungeon's floor; tore, with my nails, my hair, my flesh, my garments; groaned, howled, shrieked, in frantic agony. Towards morning, a stream of blood gushed from my nose and lips, and, mingling with a flood of tears, a kindly and copious shower, recalled me from the verge of insanity. The first collected thought which returning sense presented was, a determination to avoid the man whose value I had learned too late, and by whom I had been beloved in my days of peace and innocence. I procured, as the day advanced, the implements of writing, and traced the characters delivered to your hand; presaging, but too truly, your humane solicitude.

"'At this period, I felt suddenly awakened, as it were, to a new existence. The prospect of death, by bounding the future, threw my reflections upon the past. I indulged in the mournful retrospect; I committed it to paper;[38] while, as my thoughts were methodized, my spirit became serene.

"'Lowly and tranquil, I await my destiny; but feel, in the moment that life is cut short, dispositions springing and powers expanding, that, permitted to unfold themselves, might yet make reparation to the society I have injured, and on which I have but too well retaliated my wrongs. But it is too late! *Law* completes the triumph of injustice. The despotism of man rendered me weak, his vices betrayed me into shame, a barbarous policy stifled returning dignity, prejudice robbed me of the means of independence, gratitude ensnared me in the devices of treachery, the contagion of example corrupted my heart, despair hardened and brutality rendered it cruel. A sanguinary policy precludes reformation, defeating the dear-bought lessons of experience, and, by a legal process, assuming the arm of omnipotence, annihilates the being whom its negligence left destitute, and its institutions compelled to offend.

"'Thou, also, it may be, art incapable of distinction; thou, too, probably, hast bartered the ingenuous virtues, the sensibility of youth, for the despotism, the arrogance, the voluptuousness of man, and the unfortunate daughter of an abandoned and wretched mother will spread to thee her innocent arms in vain. If, amidst the corruption of vaunted civilization, thy heart can yet throb responsive to the voice of nature, and yield to the claims of humanity, snatch from destruction the child of an illicit commerce, shelter her infant purity from contagion, guard her helpless youth from a pitiless world, cultivate her reason, make her feel her nature's worth, strengthen her faculties, inure her to suffer hardship, rouse her to independence, inspire her with fortitude, with energy, with self-respect, and teach her to contemn the tyranny that would impose fetters of sex upon her mind.

"'MARY.'"

Mr. Raymond, in continuation: —

"The cover of these papers contained directions whereby I might trace the unhappy orphan thus solemnly committed to my charge: it was thee, my beloved Mary! child of infamy and calamity! whom I rescued from the hovel of poverty and disgrace! I wept over thy infant beauties; I treasured up the dying precepts of thy ill-fated mother; I watched thy childhood with tender care, and nurtured thee with more than parental solicitude. It is now that I expect to reap the harvest of my cares; now is the critical period arrived on which hangs the future destiny of the child. In the eye of the world, the misfortunes of your birth stain your unsullied youth: it is in the dignity of your own mind that you must seek resource. The father of your lover has deeply imbibed these barbarous prejudices: the character of the son is yet wavering; his virtue untried, his principles unformed. Should he forfeit the privileges of his birth and rank, — should he contemn the dazzling advantages which fortune presents to him, — should he, impelled by the fervent passions of youth, impose upon himself fetters which, once rivetted, death only can dissolve, — will avarice, will ambition, never revive in his heart? will he live untainted in the midst of contagion? will established customs and sanctioned opinions, will the allurements of pleasure and the deceptions of fashion, assail in vain his flexible youth? will he, amidst the contempt of his equals, the scorn of his superiors, support a virtuous and rational singularity? will William Pelham, in the heart of a profligate age, act the beardless philosopher? will he never become *a man of the world*? will he never curse the charms that blinded him to his interest? and may not the sensible, the virtuous, the high-souled, Mary, perceive herself, when too late, the insulted wife of the man she loves?

"RAYMOND." —

Chapter XIII

I PERUSED THIS FATAL NARRATIVE with mingled and indescribable emotion. I re-perused it: it was long ere I was capable of fully comprehending the consequences it involved: — by degrees they became unfolded to me in their extent; and this first lesson of injustice swelled my heart with indignant agony. It is thus that the principles of ingenuous youth, on his entrance into the world, become bewildered and shaken. Assailed by prejudice, betrayed by sophistry, distracted by contradiction, entangled in error, he exchanges the simple dictates of artless youth, the generous feelings of an uncorrupted heart, the warm glow of natural affections, for the jargon of superstition, the frigid precautions of selfishness, the mask of hypocrisy, and the factitious distinctions of capricious folly: reason is perverted and fettered, and virtue polluted at its source.

I remained in my chamber for some hours, buried in thought, till I was roused from my rêverie by some one softly opening the door. I started; the packet fell from my lap; and, on beholding William gazing earnestly in my face, (on which the recent traces of passion were legibly impressed,) with apparent surprise and concern. I burst into a convulsive flood of tears. Covering my face with my handkerchief, and pointing to the manuscript, which lay scattered on the floor, I rushed by him, and fled precipitately from the apartment, while, having collected the papers, William retired with them to his chamber.

Feeling a sense of oppression, almost to suffocation, I quitted the house, and wandered, unconscious of my path, into an adjoining copse, till the night shut in, dark and stormy. The wind howled mournfully through the foliage; the leaves were scattered at my feet; the rain fell in

71

torrents, cold and chill; the underwood caught and rent my garments, which clung around me, heavy with the damps, and impeded my progress. I experienced, in encountering the conflicting elements, a gloomy species of pleasure: they were, methought, less rude and savage than barbarous man. I recalled to my remembrance the image of my wretched mother: I beheld her, in idea, abandoned to infamy, cast out of society, stained with blood, expiring on a scaffold, unpitied and unwept. I clasped my hands in agony; terrors assailed me till then unknown; the blood froze in my veins; a shuddering horror crept through my heart; when a low rustling sound, from an adjoining thicket, suddenly caught my startled ear; while a pale light gleamed at intervals through the trees. Listening, in fearful, undefinable, expectancy, my breath grew short, my heart palpitated laboriously, seeming to swell to my throat, as I essayed in vain to shriek. The sounds at length became more distinct; hasty footsteps approached; while, fatigued with unusual exertion, chilled by the hostile elements, which every moment grew more tempestuous, agitated by terrible and nameless emotions, exhausted by the struggle of warring passions, my strength and my spirits utterly failed, and I sunk without motion on the turf.

Returning, in a few moments, to life and recollection, I found myself in the arms of my lover, accompanied by Mr. Neville, and a servant carrying a light, to assist them in their search through the dark and pathless wilderness, where, alarmed by my unusual absence, and the inclemency of the weather, they had, for some time, sought me in vain.

"For God's sake! my dear Miss Raymond!" exclaimed my host, in a tone of mingled kindness and reproach, "what could induce you to prolong your walk in a night like this? You know not the anxiety you have caused us."

"I thank you," replied I, in a faint voice, "for your friendly concern. I had, I believe, missed my path."

William's eyes were fixed earnestly upon mine. Withdrawing myself from his arms, which still supported me, and accepting the aid of Mr. Neville, I returned with languid steps towards the house. Mrs. Neville, on our entrance, hastened to meet us, full of solicitude on my account. Observing in my countenance the traces of unusual emotion, she accosted me with tender sympathy, pressing me to retire, and take that repose which I so evidently required. Attending me to my chamber, she assisted in disengaging me from my wet garments. A torpid pain oppressed my head; lassitude and restlessness seized my limbs; cold shiverings, succeeded by a feverish disorder, confined me for some days to my apartment. During my indisposition, I was attended by my hostess with maternal care. Assuring her that my disorder would be but transient, I sought to calm her inquietude, and obtained from her a promise that my guardian, without a material and threatening change, should not be alarmed by the knowledge of my situation.

My lover, abandoning himself for some days to the most lively affliction, would not be excluded from my chamber; sitting or kneeling whole hours in silence near the feet of my bed, his arms folded, and his features expressive of the most poignant grief. My disorder at length abating, my spirits grew more tranquil. At my earnest request, William was prevailed upon to quit my apartment, and to content himself with short occasional visits and frequent inquiries. In my present feeble state, I convinced him, the discomposure I suffered from his presence was peculiarly injurious. I solicited and obtained from him the return of the fatal packet, which I had promised to confide to my kind hostess; and I engaged, on my recovery, to discuss with him its contents.

During my state of convalescence, I had time for reflection. The languor remaining from the effects of my illness abated the fervour of my feelings: the endearing tenderness of my friend, who, with lively sympathy, interested herself in my situation, her judicious counsels, and animated approbation of my principles and conduct, aided, flattered, and soothed, me; while her experience enlightened me respecting the nature of those customs of which I had previously formed but a confused apprehension. My resolutions every hour acquired strength, and my mind regained its vigour: I became inspired with an emulation to prove myself worthy the confidence of my patron, who, satisfied with having communicated to me the circumstances which rendered my destiny peculiar, trusted for my conduct to the principles he had impressed upon my mind; principles, of which he had a right to expect the fruits.

Chapter XIV

MY LOVER GREW IMPATIENT for the promised conference; a conference, how dreaded soever, which, my health being now nearly re-established, I had no longer any pretence to avoid.

"Why," said he, in a tone of reproach, as he entered the parlour, where I waited in agitation his approach, "why am I excluded from your presence? Why, when we meet, those averted eyes, that cold and distant air? Can it be that the tender, the sensible, Mary hesitates whether to sacrifice the man who adores her, the man whom she has a thousand times professed to love, to a senseless chimera, an odious tyranny, against which reason indignantly revolts; or does she delight to torture the heart, over which she is but too well assured of her power?"

"Alas, my friend!" replied I, regarding him with melancholy earnestness, and gently placing my hand on his, which he vehemently snatched to his lips, "wound not my heart by these injurious reproaches. It is true that *I love you*, tenderly love you: God knows how dear you are to me, and the anguish it costs me to be compelled to renounce you! God knows that, in rending from my heart the sentiment so cherished, the sentiment that has so long constituted its happiness, I part with all that endears life!"

"Why, then, do violence to that invaluable heart? Why not listen to its just and gentle dictates?"

"Need I recall to your mind" (covering my face with my handkerchief) "the tale which has harrowed up my own? Ah, William! can I, ought I, to bring dishonour as my only dowry to the arms of the man I love?"

"You deceive yourself, Mary, when you would adopt the language which truth and nature alike abhor. Beauty, virtue, talents, derive honour from no station, and confer it upon all. Can a mind enlightened, a spirit dignified, as your's, submit to a tyranny thus fantastic?"

"I do not deny that I am sensible of its injustice; an injustice that my reason and my affections equally contemn; yet who am I, that I should resist the united voice of mankind, that I should oppose a judgement immature and inexperienced against the customs which use has sanctioned, and expedience, it may be, confirmed?"

"Are there the magnanimous principles, is this the fortitude, that blended respect with tenderness, that left my heart in doubt whether the passion you inspired — "

"Ah! I know too well all you would urge: I dare not trust your pleadings; I dread lest I should mistake the temerity of passion for the dictates of principle, lest I should purchase present gratification at the expense of future remorse."

"And what is the dreaded, the chimerical, evil, to avert which demands this expensive sacrifice; to which you thus lavishly offer up our dearest hopes? — Duty, virtue, happiness, form an indissoluble bond. Can it be you, rash, but charming, maid! who seek, by factitious distinctions, to dissolve the sacred union?"

"Our situations, our claims, our prospects, thus widely differing, dare I entail upon you evils to which your firmness and your recompense might, alas! be unequal?"

"You love me not:" (his cheeks glowing and his eyes flashing fire:) "did you love me, these suspicions, so unworthy of yourself and your lover, would have no place in your heart. I perceive but too plainly that you distrust and despise me!"

"My friend! my beloved friend! your emotion afflicts, but does not offend me. Have pity on my weakness, on my youth, my sex. My heart sinks under the task imposed upon it: in afflicting you, heaven knows the anguish it endures. Distinguish, I entreat you, distinguish between our various duties In mo, it is virtue to submit to a destiny, however painful, not wilfully incurred; and, in all that affects myself merely, to rise magnanimously above it: but why should *you* expose yourself to a doubtful conflict and a certain penalty? — The confidence which in you is generous, in me would change its nature, and, in its failure, entail upon me a double portion of remorse and shame. — William, dear William, turn not thus from me! Your displeasure pierces my soul."

"My dearest girl! distract me not thus with contradictions and refinements; suffer not the simplicity of your mind to be perverted and debauched by factitious sophisms; do not yield our mutual happiness to the subtleties of a fantastic theory."

"Answer me, my friend, and answer me truly, dare you believe that your father, tenacious of the honour of an unsullied name, would consent to our union, would consent to enrol a daughter of infamy in a family vain of illustrious descent? Have the habits of your youth inured you to labour? have they prepared you for independence? Have reprobation, poverty, disgrace, the contumely of the world, however unmerited, no terrors for William Pelham? Will he forfeit the privileges of his rank and birth? Will he, for the smiles of love, brave the frowns of fortune, and, in the decay of those charms, which owe to youth and novelty their gloss, will he never repent, will he never curse, the fascination which misled him to his ruin?"

"Why thus conjure up phantoms for our mutual torture? Where is the necessity for combating evils thus formidably and fancifully arrayed? The cruel narrative, that has wounded your gentle nature, is probably known but to ourselves: the village believes you the relation of your patron; my father knows you for no other: by a prudent silence, the consequences of its disclosure might yet be averted. My father loves me: he is not sordid: why should we rouse in his heart this idol, honour? Is it virtue to sacrifice to the shrine of prejudice, however venerable or imposing its claims?"

"Dare you then believe that my guardian, whose stern integrity bends to no expedients, could be prevailed upon to foster the deceit? On a subject thus interesting, would Mr. Pelham make no inquiries, should we consent to unite in a wilful prevarication? Is there no cause to fear lest the voice of rumour, that blazons the tale of shame, should bear the cruel tidings to his ear?"

"What is the value of *truth*, abstracted from its expedience? — Virtue itself is worthless but as a mean to *happiness*."

"Ah! beware of sophistry and conscious perversion! A present gratification in view, is there no danger of selfish delusion? Is passion an impartial judge of the propriety of violating moral sanctions? If, where interest assails us, we suffer our principles to yield, who can tell to what fearful lengths, on lesser occasions, a precedent thus pernicious may lead us! — Is a habit of rectitude broken with impunity?"

"Good God!" exclaimed my lover, with vehemence, "does *love* argue thus coolly when its dearest interests are at stake? You love me not! you never loved me! Pride and fickleness have fortified your heart! It is vain to expect from woman a stability for which sex and nature have incapacitated her!"

"Unjust William! cruel as unjust! what but *love*, tender, powerful, self-annihilating love, — that, where the welfare of the beloved object is at stake, triumphing in its sufferings, is content to be the victim, — could enable me to

78

stifle the importunate yearnings of a fond and breaking heart? I perceive on every side, while I would ward them from you, the miseries which menace our ill-fated attachment. A dark cloud, surcharged with storms, hangs over my fate. Let it waste on me its fury. I dare to give you up, to lose, to renounce you. I can weep, and my sorrow shall be luxury; but I dare not, will not, consent to involve in my destiny the man I love, — to become at once his misfortune and his curse."

My exhausted spirits would no longer sustain me: my head sunk on my bosom, my tears flowed without control. My lover knelt at my feet, folded me to his bosom, tenderly embraced me, mingling his tears with mine, and at length wrung from me a promise that I would consent to be his, if, after disclosing to his father, without reserve, the particulars of my birth, he could, by expostulation or entreaties, extort from him even a reluctant consent. He assured himself, with the sanguine ardour of youth and inexperience, that every scruple must be vanquished by the powerful and united eloquence of nature, love, and truth.

I listened to his rapturous exultations in mournful silence. I returned to him the papers of Mr. Raymond. Separating myself from him with difficulty, I retired to my chamber, whither I was followed by my kind hostess. Repeating to her the particulars of the past conflict, I sought relief in her tender sympathy.

Early in the ensuing morning, William departed for the metropolis. I presaged but too well the issue of his romantic project, and a fearful despondency gradually pervaded my mind.

Chapter XV

ON THE FOLLOWING DAY, as my thoughts became more collected, I took up my pen, and, addressing myself to Mr. Raymond, made him a faithful recital of the circumstances
which had succeeded the receipt of his affecting narrative.
I poured out my heart to this invaluable friend without reserve, and besought his future counsel.

"You have fulfilled, my dearest child," said he, in his
reply to my appeal, "my most sanguine expectation. Con-
tinue to act up to the dictates of your own admirable
judgement: if I had not assisted you in forming principles
of rectitude, and in acquiring courage to put them in practice, I should not now dare to add, to the crime of negligence, the tyranny of control. It is *you* who are to decide
on the materials laid before you; but do not misconstrue
the grounds of my solicitude; there is no contradiction in
the principles I would inculcate. Your affection for William Pelham, not more natural than laudable, has hitherto
produced upon your character the happiest effects: virtuous tenderness purifies the heart, carries forward the understanding, refines the passions, dignifies the feelings,
and raises human nature to its sublimest standard of excellence. I rejoice in your capacity for these admirable
sensibilities; but, when I perceive you exalted, but not enslaved by them, I exult and glory in my child! William's
youth, inexperience, instability, and habits of dependence,
are the only reasonable obstacles which oppose your mutual wishes: should his attachment prove worthy its object,
these obstacles, though threatening, are far from insuperable. His destiny will not permit us to confine him i● rural
shades: let him try the world, and prove his boasted
strength: if, in the arduous warfare, victory crown his ef-

forts, let him return, and claim the recompense of his toils: the invaluable heart of my child will be a victor's rich reward

"I yearn to clasp my beloved Mary, the pride and comfort of my declining years, to my paternal bosom. In her happiness and improvement, my hopes and affections fondly centre.

"RAYMOND."

The concluding paragraph of this letter determined me on an immediate return to the beloved asylum of my childhood. The necessity for my absence no longer existed: I longed to embrace my father and my friend, to bask in the sunshine of his approving smiles. After acquainting my friends with my intention, I began with alacrity to prepare for my departure.

The evening previous to the day appointed for my journey, a letter was brought by a horseman to the parsonage, superscribed to Miss Raymond. I had strayed into the meadows adjoining the orchard, and met, on my return, my hostess, who had been seeking me, and who put into my hand the paper left by the messenger. I trembled and changed colour on recognizing the well-known writing of my lover. Hastily breaking the seal, I read the following lines: —

"*To* MISS RAYMOND.

"Your mistaken heroism has ruined us! My father is inexorable! He is preparing to send me to the continent, whither Edmund is, for the benefit of his health, advised to repair. Two years is the period allotted for our absence. I am determined to resist this tyranny, and brave every consequence. I shall follow my letter immediately, and once more tender to you my heart and hand: if you are then resolved rather to obey the dictates of a frigid prudence than yield to the united claims of virtue, love, and reason, you will probably regret in future the effects of a despair for which *you* only will be responsible.

"W.P."

The fortitude I had been struggling to attain forsook me on the perusal of this epistle. I gave it, without speaking, to my friend, and, clasping my arms round her neck, sunk, half-fainting, on her maternal bosom. She supported me to my chamber, and, remaining with me till the night was far spent, sought by every endearment to calm the perturbation of my spirits. Quitting me towards morning, she entreated me to endeavour to take some repose. In compliance with her solicitude, I threw myself, in my clothes, on the bed, but rest fled from me. As the day dawned, abandoning my pillow, and softly stealing from my chamber, I panted to relieve my overcharged heart by breathing a freer air. Opening the door which led into the garden, I wandered through the enclosures, and, at length, wearied and exhausted, seated myself on a rustic bench, at the foot of an aged oak, where I watched the crimson clouds, the harbingers of day. Absorbed in reflection, the hours passed unheeded, and the sun rose high above the horizon ere I quitted my retreat.

I returned slowly towards the house, and, on entering the parlour, beheld, with surprise and emotion, my lover in earnest conversation with Mrs. Neville, his dress negligent and his air wild and perturbed. He turned suddenly, on my entrance, and, observing my pallid countenance, tottering steps, and features on which the ravages of passion were impressed, folded me to his bosom, and, by the mute eloquence of affectionate endearment, expressed his tender sympathy. The entrance of Mr. Neville prevented for the present any explanation of our sentiments. During the repast, I tried to rally my fainting spirits, and to prepare myself for the approaching trial. I recalled to my remembrance every consideration which might tend to fortify my conduct and control my feelings, while I sought in vain to rouse my languid powers. Our humane host but too well comprehending our situation, on some pretence, breakfast being ended, quitted the room. Mrs. Neville was about to follow her husband, but, preventing her design, I entreated the support of her presence.

In vain should I attempt to do justice to the conflict which ensued: my lover omitted no means to effect his purpose and assail my faultering resolution: he knelt, implored, argued, wept, threatened, reproached; cursed himself, his father, my patron, the whole world, with terrible imprecations; gave a loose to all the impetuosity of his passions; and abandoned himself to the most frantic excesses. Stunned, confounded, shocked, overborne, my senses grew bewildered: I sunk into a kind of stupor, and became unconscious to what was passing. I neither spoke nor wept; but, with a wild air, continued to gaze vacantly.

Mrs. Neville perceived my situation; and, taking my cold and lifeless hand, attempted to withdraw me from a scene to which my faculties were no longer equal. She uttered, as she tried to rouse my attention, a severe reprimand to my lover. He caught the alarm, checked himself, and, at her repeated solicitation, consented to withdraw, and to postpone for the present what he had farther to urge.

It was not till after many hours, and a short but profound slumber, that I was capable of resuming the affecting subject. William, apprehensive for my health and intellects, had now become more moderate: he at length suffered himself to yield to our united reasonings, respecting the danger and impropriety of a precipitate conduct, in defiance of his father's injunctions, in a case thus important. I communicated to him the letter I had received from Mr. Raymond, wherein he generously confides in my judgement and prudence, and hints, that the barriers, which, at present, opposed themselves to our happiness, may yield to time and perseverance. I assured my lover, repeatedly and tenderly assured him, if, on his return from the continent, a commerce with the world had wrought no change in his affections; if, in the interval, he had determined on some plan of independence; if, when not wholly unacquainted with them, he persisted in despising the allurements of interest and ambition; if his present views and sentiments were confirmed and sanctioned by time and experience; he might then challenge my faith and affection, and I should glory in aiding him to give an example to the world of the triumph of virtuous and unsophisticated feelings.

Appeased, in some measure, by these representations, he engaged in all things to resign himself to my will, on condition that I would previously, as a pledge of my sincerity, and to obviate future hazards or plans for our separation, suffer the nuptial-ceremony to be performed by Mr. Neville: in that case, whatever it might cost him, he would quit me immediately after the service, would go abroad, remain there the allotted period, and endeavour to wait patiently a prudent season for the disclosure of our marriage.

"Do you not perceive, my friend," replied I, "the inconsistency, the absurdity, of this plan? — What! shall I first bind my fate to your's, and then suffer you, far from the influence of my tender, watchful, affection, to expose your yet-uncertain virtue to the contagion of the world?"

"Promise me, then," interrupted he, with vehemence, "promise that, in my absence, you will listen to no other proposals: I foresee the trials to which your constancy will be exposed; every man who beholds will love you, will be my rival."

"If your knowledge of my heart afford you not a security for my faith, weak indeed were the sanction of oaths, and unworthy the sacred flame that animates us: were not your fears as injurious as chimerical, would you accept the cold reluctant hand, the victim of superstition, when the alienated mind deplored the sacrifice? No, William! I will neither give nor receive vows: let us both be free, and let our re-union be the cheerful, voluntary, dignified, consummation of love and virtue."

The day wore away before the scruples of my lover were vanquished: the contention was long and arduous: I suffered not my friend to quit me for a moment, distrusting the spirit for which I had so painfully struggled. Our parting was tender and mournful: my lover quitting me, and returning again and again to take a last embrace, protracted the agony of separation. The next day and the day following, wholly absorbed in grief, I was unable to quit my chamber: my benefactor, my home, every idea but one seemed entirely effaced from my remembrance.

[Volume II]

Chapter I

FROM THE TENDER SORROWS occasioned by the departure of my lover, I was roused, on the third morning after our separation, by a more serious evil. I had joined my friends at the breakfast-table, and was exerting myself to take a share in the familiar affectionate effusions and greetings, which more peculiarly distinguished the early repasts of this interesting family. The children, blooming as cherubs, who had of late missed my accustomed attentions, lavishing on me their artless caresses, were exerting all the graces of infancy to obtain my notice; while Mr. and Mrs. Neville, regarding their efforts with a tender complacency, on their parts omitted no kind or soothing attention to amuse and cheer me. In the midst of this simple and friendly intercourse, the servant, entering, informed my host that a person desired to speak with him on urgent business. Instantly quitting us, he remained shut up in his study near an hour with the stranger; on whose departure, he rejoined us in the parlour, where I had continued with Mrs. Neville, engaged in an interesting, though painful, retrospect of the late events. My friend was speaking to me with some earnestness as her husband re-entered, when, turning at the sound of his well-known footsteps, she stopped suddenly, uttering a fearful exclamation.

"Good God!" said she, "what has befallen you?" and sunk back in her chair, from which she had made a vain effort to rise.

Consternation and distress were painted on the features of Mr. Neville, as, taking the hand of his wife, and silently pressing it to his lips, he tenderly hung over her.

"Speak to me, my dear Neville," continued she, wildly; "for heaven's sake, speak to me! Relieve me from these intolerable apprehensions!"

"Have you fortitude, my dear Anna, to hear of the *ruin* of our little family? Can you share the poverty of the man who feels it but for you and your children?"

Folding her arms round her husband, who strained her to his heart, and embracing him with exquisite tenderness, she wept for some minutes on his bosom: at length, regarding him affectionately, and making an effort to conquer her emotion, "I exist," said she, in a tone of bewitching softness, smiling through her tears, "but for my Neville and the dear pledges of his love. With them, all situations are comparatively indifferent, – without them, all alike would be insupportable."

"You will then, perhaps, bear to hear, that I must resign my curacy, our cottage, and little farm. A week only is allowed for our removal, and God knows what is to become of us afterwards!"

My friend, for a moment, appeared shocked and confounded; but, instantly recovering herself, she assumed an air of patient resignation. "Whence this change?" interrogated she. "How have we incurred the displeasure of the rector? What is the nature of our offence?"

Mr. Neville glanced his eye slightly towards me: there was in it an expression of concern mingled with benignity. "The rector is dead!" replied he to the questions of his wife. "His advanced age and infirm health have long prepared me for such an event. Mr. Dornville, in whose gift the living is, and who had allowed me to hope for the reversion, has parted with the presentation to a gentleman to whom he is under pecuniary obligations, and who is, I suspect, willing to accept this privilege in lieu of a debt of honour; and a new incumbent has already taken possession of the rectory."

"Why, then, not apply to him? It is possible, though

we must no longer hope for the living, that the curacy and parsonage, where we have spent so many delightful hours, may still be continued to us, in consideration of your family, your merit, and long establishment." (Mr. Neville sighed and turned away his face.) "What is the name of the person at present nominated? and who is the gentleman to whom the right of presentation has been transferred?"

Mr. Neville was still silent. My friend repeated and pressed her question. "*Sir Peter Osborne,*" at length, replied he emphatically.

The sound produced upon my frame an electric effect. Starting from the seat, where I had hitherto remained in anxious attention, — gasping for breath, and clasping my hands in agony, — I sunk on my knees at the feet of my friends, my supplicating eyes lifted towards them. Struggling for utterance, which, for a moment, seemed denied me,

"It is to me, then," at last I exclaimed, "wretched child of misfortune! that you owe this calamity; me, who am fated to involve in my destiny all who know or love me!"

Raising me tenderly, they embraced and soothed me, delicately appearing in my concern to lose the sense of their own disappointment; but it was long ere my spirits regained any degree of composure. My host, in the course of the day, informed us, that the messenger who had brought him these unpleasant tidings was the steward of Mr. Dornville; that his master, having learnt the intentions of Sir Peter Osborne and the present incumbent to deprive Mr. Neville of the curacy, had expressed some compunction on the occasion, and had commissioned his steward to offer his interest to procure him the chaplainship of a garrison abroad, should he be willing to quit his country; intimating, at the same time, that, in case of his acceptance of this proposal, the expenses of fitting out, fees of office, removing his family, and other necessary charges, would amount to, at least, from three to five hundred pounds; but, if enabled to raise this sum, the appointment would well repay the trouble and expenditure. "But where," added my host, "were we inclined to accept this offer, are we to procure the money? The salary of the curacy, and the profits of the few acres annexed to the parsonage, were barely sufficient, with the utmost frugality, to support my family: some expenses I have incurred in the improvement of my land: and, when our hay is sold, and our wheat threshed and disposed of, I doubt, after discharging the few debts which we have been obliged to contract, whether we shall have twenty pounds remaining in the world."

"We are not certain," said Mrs. Neville, after pausing for some time, "that Sir Peter is our determined enemy. As a gentleman and a man of education, he cannot be devoid of humanity: I think it would be right, at least it would be affording him no pretence against us, to make the customary application."

"To give you satisfaction, I am willing to take this step, though, I confess, it is with some reluctance, after the specimen we have had of his character in his ungentleman-like persecutions of Miss Raymond, and the irritable state of mind in which he last left our house. These recollections much incline me, I own, to suspect, in this affair, a deliberate plan of malice; nevertheless, as I would leave no means, consistent with what is due to my own character, untried, when the welfare of my family is at stake, I will adopt the conduct you propose; but I will not humble myself to a man of a temper so apparently ferocious and malignant."

In consequence of this resolution, a messenger was

dispatched to the rector, who returned, in a short time, with a letter coldly civil, informing my friend, that he had already pledged his word for the curacy to a person recommended by his patron, to whom he referred Mr. Neville's messenger. To this reference Sir Peter Osborne had also vouchsafed a reply equally characteristic and insulting: — That Mr. Neville would have done well to have employed the agency of his guest, Miss Raymond, on this occasion, to whose intercession he was greatly disposed to listen. — A transient emotion of anger, to which he disdained to give words, flashed in the eyes of my host, and glowed on his cheek, as he perused this barbarous sarcasm; while my feelings were those of bitter, unmixed, anguish. My friends, ever amiable and magnanimous, suppressed, in consideration of my share in the misfortune, the expression of their own just sensations on so cruel a change in their situation and prospects.

I could not be prevailed upon to leave them till I had assisted Mrs. Neville in the melancholy employment of removing their simple furniture to a neighbouring hamlet. In these trying circumstances, she exerted herself with a patient cheerfulness truly admirable and heroic; endeavouring, by every tender attention, even, at times, by sprightly sallies, to divert the dejection that clouded the aspect of her husband, and to cheer the still deeper depression which weighed down my spirits, from a reflection on the occasion of this melancholy change. My thoughts no longer fondly dwelt on my lover; I scarcely recollected that he was in existence; my whole attention was concentred in the calamities of this excellent pair, while I revolved in my mind a thousand vague plans for their relief and future establishment. At length, becoming impatient to communicate my projects to my dear father and monitor, on whose wisdom and kindness I felt the most perfect reliance, and to consult him on a subject thus heavily pressing on my heart, after seeing my friends settled in their new abode, I quitted them with regret, and returned, with a mind, alas! how changed, to the once-happy scenes of my childhood.

A tide of recollections gushed upon my heart as I entered the dear parental asylum. Mr. Raymond folded me to his bosom in speechless emotion. I wept in his arms, and an eloquent silence of some minutes ensued. Methought, as I gazed upon his venerable countenance, it appeared overspread with wanness; the features were sunk and changed. A slight expression of disappointment seemed blended with the concern and tenderness which were painted in his eyes, as, gently tapping my cheek,

"Where are the roses," said he, in a tone affectedly sportive, yet half-reproachful, "that once blossomed on the cheek of my Mary? I had flattered myself that my girl would have risen superior to this love-sick weakness."

A suffusion of scarlet dyed my face and neck. "Nor have you deceived yourself, my father! Far other cares at present occupy my thoughts." I proceeded minutely to relate to him the preceding events, of which my mind was full, while he listened to my narration with evident and lively emotion.

"And what, my child," said he, as I concluded, "is to be done? What would you wish me to do?"

"Rescue, if possible, this amiable family from the fate that awaits them."

He paused for some time: at length, regarding me with a countenance of affectionate solicitude, "This is, indeed," resumed he, "an unfortunate circumstance; it affects me more than I am able to express. I can conceive but of one resource, and on that I scarcely dare to think."

"Name it," said I, grasping his hand eagerly, and fixing

on his my inquiring eyes.

He hesitated, sighed, and, in a faultering accent, at length continued: "Can Mary encounter the perils of indigence? Is that delicate frame fitted for labour?"

"How, my dear sir! for heaven's sake, explain yourself!"

He proceeded with more firmness. "The principal part of my income, consisting of life-annuities, will, of course, perish with me. I have, by frugality, contrived to lay up from my annual expenses the sum of five hundred pounds, which I had destined as a small independence for my child: less than this will not extricate my friend, to whose misfortune we have unhappily, though innocently, been instrumental. I am at a loss on what to resolve: my heart is divided and torn between pressing and contending duties."

"Ah! then," exclaimed I, in a tone of ecstasy, throwing myself on the neck of my patron, "let me decide. I am young, active, healthy, and able to labour: my own error was the original cause of this calamity; it is reasonable and just that I should pay the forfeit: I have with *you* no wants; the future is uncertain and may bring with it its own resources, the present distress is immediate and admits of no delay. Afford me, I entreat you, my father, my friend," added I, with fervour, embracing him again and again, "the exquisite pleasure of relieving our unfortunate friends."

Mr. Raymond sat for some time absorbed in meditation: his sighs were frequent and profound, tears trickled through his fingers as he held his hand to his forehead: he turned his face half from me; his frame seemed shaken by internal agitation. Hanging upon him, I ceased not to importune him to abide by my decision: I already anticipated with sanguine delight the re-instating my friends in their former felicity: I continued, with increasing vehemence, to reiterate my arguments and entreaties, till my kind guardian, vanquished by this zeal and perseverance, yielded to my wishes, and consented to resign to my disposal the contested sum.

"Take it," said he, "Mary," emphatically, as he put into my hands a draught for the amount, "and do with it according to the liberal dictates of your own noble mind. May the period never arrive when my child may have cause to rue her lavish generosity!"

So much apparent regret mingled with this action of Mr. Raymond, that, had I not, in a thousand instances, witnessed his even lavish benevolence, had I not been assured of his sympathy in the misfortunes of his friends, had I not imputed his concern to its true source, affection for me and solicitude for my welfare, my heart would have felt inclined to reproach the reluctant, ungrateful, donation. It was with difficulty I could chase, by lively sallies and playful caresses, the cloud that had fixed itself on his brow.

Seeming to regard me with looks of mingled tenderness and compassion, he frequently averted his face, as if to hide the starting tear. I consulted with him respecting the most delicate and proper method of effecting our purpose, and we determined on an anonymous conveyance, as a mean the least liable to scruple or defeat.

Chapter II

AIDED BY THE SECRET BOUNTY of my guardian, Mr. Neville signified to Mr. Dornville his acceptance of the foreign appointment, which, on inquiry, appeared to be combined with circumstances peculiarly promising. He began to make preparations for his departure; but, before he quitted the country, agreed to pass with us some days, at the united request of Mr. Raymond and myself. Our separation was solemn and affecting: my friends spoke with regret of their ignorance of their benefactor, on whom they lavished blessings and acknowledgements. Mrs. Neville pressed me to her maternal bosom: I caressed and wept over the children. We parted with reciprocal assurances of tender recollection and mutual wishes for a reunion.

During these events, I had received frequent letters from my lover, (letters breathing the most passionate tenderness,) who, with his brother, had quitted England, and had taken the route to Paris. My benefactor, to whose perusal I offered these endearing proofs of the affection and fidelity of my friend, put them back with a rejecting hand.

"To her own prudence and virtue I commit my child" (for, so he delighted to call me:) "the delicacies of affection are prophaned by common or indifferent eyes: of my girl I have no distrust: may William prove worthy of her!"

As the tumult which had lately disquieted my spirits gradually subsided, I had more leisure to contemplate the ravages which disease, rather than age, had made on the strength of my first and best friend. An acute disorder, to which he had for a long period been liable, now returned more frequently, and the paroxysms were of longer duration. This circumstance, added to the painful emotions which appeared to agitate him on the slightest allusion to the subject, prevented me from touching on the narrative of my unfortunate mother. There seemed to have been a tacit compact between us to avoid any reference to what must have proved mutually painful. As his malady increased, his patience and fortitude, amidst trying pangs, were a constant and impressive lesson. My time, my cares, and my attentions, were wholly devoted to him.

At this period, the return of Sir Peter Osborne to the country gave me new vexation and alarm. He renewed his persecutions with a disgusting audacity, insulted me with licentious proposals, contrived various methods of conveying to me offers of a splendid settlement, and reduced me to the necessity of confining myself wholly to the house. At length, frustrated in his attempts and inflamed by opposition, he changed his conduct, professed honourable views, and, under this pretence, obtained, with some difficulty, an audience of Mr. Raymond, whose interest he deigned to solicit, and before whom he made an ostentatious display of his ample possessions and liberal intentions in my favour. My patron engaged to relate to me the particulars of the interview, disclaiming any other interference.

At the same time, a humbler destiny offered itself to my acceptance: a neighbouring farmer, young, honest, simple, industrious, and moderately wealthy, solicited, with rustic praises and artless professions of regard and admiration, my heart and hand.

"What say you, Mary?" added my kind friend, after reporting to me these different pretensions. "I would fain see my girl in a safe and sheltered situation before I resign my existence; a period which my various infirmities warn me can be at no great distance." I looked at him, and my eyes involuntarily filled with tears. "I understand you," said he, while his own eyes glistened. Taking my hand, and unaffectedly smiling, "I need no assurances of your love Approaching dissolution has no terrors for me: I have, I hope, fulfilled my destiny, and of my duties have not been wholly negligent: I have experienced some sorrows, but more enjoyments: your improvements and perfections have added greatly to the sum of the latter, as a care for your future welfare is now my only remaining anxiety."

"Surely, my dear sir, you can be in no suspense as to the sentiments of my heart, much less respecting my opinions of Sir Peter Osborne. Can the mind you have formed be allured by sordid motives to desert its principles?"

"I hope not. Certainly I had no doubts upon this subject, but merely spoke of it in conformity to my engagement with Sir Peter. But what shall I say to my honest friend the farmer? A life of agriculture has many advantages: it is natural, active, healthful, and, in a great degree, independent: it affords intervals for social enjoyment and the cultivation of the mind, and is favourable to virtue: methinks I could like to see my girl grace the dairy; she would make the prettiest dairy-maid in the county."

I sighed; I felt my colour change; my eyes fell under those of my guardian, who regarded me with smiling earnestness. I continued silent.

"How am I to interpret those sighs, that changing countenance, and those downcast looks?"

"*I love William Pelham*, sir: shall I give my hand without my heart?"

He paused for some moments. At length, as if from a sudden recollection, "Tell me, Mary," resumed he, "when did you hear last from William?"

"Not lately;" hesitating, "not very lately."

"And his last letter — ."

97

"Was," turning aside to hide a starting tear, "was shorter, was — yes, I fear, I believe — less animated — less tender — " Unable to proceed, I threw my arms round the neck of my guardian, hid my face, and sobbed in his bosom.

He pressed me tenderly to his heart.

"Poor child! and so thou wouldst sacrifice future peace and usefulness to a romantic notion of the heroism of constancy." I started, hastily withdrawing myself from his paternal embrace. "I will not deceive thee, my love! I have certain intelligence that William Pelham enters into the gaieties and licentious pleasures of Paris with all the ardour that belongs to his age and character. The impressions of virtuous affection, which he received in his youth, are, probably, even by this time, effaced in the riot of voluptuous gratification. I could wish to see your life, while in its prime, dignified, active, and useful: I should sink into the grave in affliction and disappointment, were I to behold the youth and fine qualities of my child consumed by the canker of romantic sorrow and unavailing regret. Few marriages are formed on what is called *love*, in its appropriate sense; it is a bewitching, but delusive, sentiment; it dwells in the imagination, and frequently has little other connection with the object. The true beauty, of which the lover is enamoured, is merely ideal; an exquisite enchantment, dissolving on a nearer approach; an intoxicating species of enthusiasm, that (like every other extraordinary ebullition of the spirits,) subsiding, leaves them proportionably exhausted. The mind incapable of these elevated conceptions wants vigour; the mind subdued by them is weak. The sentiments you have experienced have increased the worth of your character: an irresistible charm is added by these graceful sensibilities to the attractions of youth, but your peculiar destiny calls

for severer exertions: shake off, then, this enervating softness, and live henceforward to *reason* and *virtue*."

"Allow me time, my father! my friend!" exclaimed I,
in a voice half-stifled with emotion, struggling to conceal
my anguish; "allow me time to wean my mind from the
feelings which have so long constituted its happiness and
its glory. Should William indeed prove unworthy of my
tenderness, my heart, if it break not, shall be taught to
bend to the dictates of reason; but do not compel me to
be unjust, do not let your rational and laudable concern
for my welfare betray you into tyranny. I cannot, I ought
not, to bestow on any man a reluctant hand with an alienated heart. It is not necessary that I should marry; I
can exert my talents for my support, or procure a sustenance by the labour of my hands.[39] I dare encounter indigence; but I dare not prostitute my sincerity and my
faith."

"Alas!" replied my patron, regarding me significantly,
and shaking his head with a distrustful air, "alas! you are
ignorant of the world and its corruptions! To leave you
so young, so lovely, so friendless, plants in my heart a
thousand daggers. But I urge you not, my love! Take time
to reflect, and weigh all that has passed."

With this permission I retired to my chamber. When
alone, I revolved, in silence and in solitude, the new apprehensions which poured, in a torrent, upon my heart.
"William is unfaithful! William is corrupted!" I exclaimed
in agony, while scalding tears gushed from my eyes. "A
few short months have effaced from his remembrance
those impressions which I fondly persuaded myself would
be indelible, would guard his heart as with an impenetra-
ble aegis! He has forgotten his Mary; she who lived but
for him alone! He is already (oh, fatal prediction!) become
a *man of the world*!" My imagination called up and dwelt

upon a thousand racking, torturing, images: William dissipating himself in thoughtless frivolity, indulging in voluptuous riot, forgetful of Mary, of love, of virtue! Till this fatal period, some sweet ingredient had mingled in my cup of sorrow, some flattering hope whispered, in seraph's accents, peace to my wounded spirit – but *now* all was bitter, unmixed, corrosive, agony! The fabric of rare felicity, which fancy had busied itself in erecting, sunk, at once, on its airy foundation, and left a dreary, a desolate, void. Days succeeded each other, black and joyless: a tempest of passions raged in my heart, and swept before it my feeble reason: the light of day became hateful to me: I secluded myself in solitary and distant apartments, avoiding the presence of my patron, whose looks, though he spoke not, seemed to reprove me.

At length, exhausted by their excess, my emotions began to subside. I remembered that my lover existed not alone in the universe; that I had other obligations, other duties, to fulfil. A secret reproach stung my heart; I sought to rally my sinking powers; I blushed at the selfish weakness which I had suffered thus to subdue me; I struggled with my emotions, nor combated them in vain; a sense of conscious worth swelled my bosom, and elevated my feelings to a higher tone. I repeated to myself, and sought to impress it on my mind, "If William is lost to Mary, he is also lost to virtue: I lament his defection, but shall I then forfeit my mind's independence, my nature's proudest boast? – If he is senseless and criminal, shall I justify myself in weakness? No, I will be calm; I will wait patiently. Calumny may have traduced him; his lapse may be transient; virtue may regain its ascendant in his heart; but, should none of these things happen, my spirit shall struggle to free itself; nor shall it struggle in vain; the hopes of my friend and father shall not be frustrated in my weakness."¸ — My thoughts became collected and my bosom serene. I sought my guardian, unaffectedly smiling through the traces of recent tears: he had perceived the conflict, and anticipated the victory.

"It is now," said he, embracing me, "that I indeed glory in my child." — Sir Peter Osborne, he informed me, had received my rejection with rage and surprise, and poured forth a torrent of invective and brutal menaces, — "And your humbler suitor — " continued he,

"Must," interrupted I, "for the present content himself with my acknowledgements."

"For the *present*, only?"

"Yes, my dear sir; for, to whom is the future known? Yet, I frankly avow that I have no hope to afford him."

"Well, well, if it must be so, I acquiesce. if I am less sanguine and less heroic than my child, it is because I am many years older, and *experience* has been my tutor."

Repeated and painful paroxysms of the disorder which harassed my friend made hourly depredations on his constitution: patient, cheerful, active, he continued, for many months, to repel these attacks, till nature at length was foiled in the unequal contest, and dissolution rapidly drew near.

"Mary," said he, a few hours before his decease, as, leaning on his pillow, I supported him in my arms, "I feel no other struggle in resigning life but that which arises from the idea of leaving thee, my child! thus forlorn and unprotected. Among my papers is a letter received a few days since from a friend in London, a generous and worthy man, with whom I was formerly in habits of familiar intercourse. He has married, since my retirement, a woman of large fortune, a connection, which his own expensive manner of living had rendered but too necessary. With the character of his lady I am entirely unacquainted;

but he informs me, in the letter alluded to, that she wishes to engage a young person, well educated, to assist her in superintending her household and family. His own health, he adds, is but in an infirm and precarious state. — I love not, I own, these situations: I am aware of the dependence that belongs to them, and the servility to which they tend: but London is the centre to which talents and accomplishments naturally resort: in London, connections may be acquired, employment sought, observation avoided, and liberty preserved. If I have not already prepared you for the vicissitudes that may befal you, it would now be too late; yet, while I confide in your principles and habits, I tremble for your personal attractions. Preserve the manuscript which contains the fate of your unfortunate mother: I can give you no stronger lesson. Desert not yourself in any situation, however difficult and perilous: never be induced to despair; continually press forward: ever bear in mind, that on *yourself* depends the worth and the dignity of your character. The good opinion of our fellow-beings is desirable: it is connected with usefulness, and ought not to be contemned. It is to be suspected, that the young person, who affects to despise the respect of the world, has already stepped over the boundary that leads to depravity: yet reputation is but a secondary good; it wears the semblance of virtue, but, if prized before the substance, may accelerate the evil it was meant to avert. Give, to the opinion of society, (the collective judgement of individuals,) the deference it merits from a being destined to tread the same stage. Distrust, yet despise not, all notions unsupported by experience; examine them with caution, and essay their practicability: when tempted to deviate from beaten paths, beware that passion be not your guide; but, where reason and duty point, intrepidly prefer the genuine dictates of truth and virtue to vulgar plaudits and sanctioned errors, how profitable soever in appearance: the silent approbation which the heart whispers in tho hour of retrospection will repay its sacrifices, and sooth it to repose amidst the clamours of ignorance or of undistinguishing malignity. — Give me your hand, my child!" continued my beloved preceptor (as he finished his injunctions, which were repeated, though with clearness, with many intervals and much interruption, from his exhausted state; but his vigorous mind, even in nature's last struggle, seemed to triumph over his feeble frame;) "give me your hand," repeated he; "nearer, yet nearer. In my escrutoire you will find a purse, containing fifty guineas: this, with the sum which will accrue from the disposal of my furniture, is all I have to bequeath: out of it, my old servants have wages to receive, and half a year's rent is due to my landlord: I know of no other claims upon me. If I had not bestowed on you a more valuable boon, in virtuous principles and an enlightened mind, you would do well to hate my memory. Repair to London as early as possible; beware of our powerful and profligate neighbour; bear in mind your own worth; *and never be led to despond.*"

His breath grew shorter and shorter, as he spoke with increased effort and difficulty; yet his countenance was placid, and he appeared free from pain. "My friend! my more than father!" exclaimed I, sinking upon my knees by the bed-side, while my arms still supported him. More I would have said, but convulsive sobs choked my utterance. A sweet serenity beamed over his features: he rested his cold cheek on mine, and gently breathed his last.

For a period, life seemed closed over me: stretched on the green sod that covered the venerable remains of the benefactor and guide of my youth, wet with the dews of heaven, sunk in sorrow, fancy brought to remembrance the animated form, the speaking countenance, the modulated accents, the mind enriched with knowledge, the endearing qualities, the exalted virtues, the touching kindness, the varied excellences, now for ever extinct, —

"Drown'd, all drown'd,
"In that great sea which nothing disembogues."[40]

Vain man! boast not perfections which to-morrow levels with the dust! Mysterious prerogative of reason, bounded by the narrow limits of experience, that, checking thy aspirations in their sublimest flights, binds them to earth in adamantine chains!

Chapter III

AFTER PAYING THE TRIBUTE of sorrow to the memory of my friend, I began, in pursuance of his last intimation, to make preparations for my departure to the metropolis. The period appointed for the absence of my lover had now nearly elapsed: our correspondence had been gradually discontinued; every succeeding letter which I had received affording only a new conviction, by its constrained and languid style, of the cruel change, of which I could no longer affect to doubt. I rallied my fortitude and my spirits; I endeavoured to chase from my bosom the deluding visions so long, so dearly, cherished; I repelled, with severe inflexibility, the recollections that every moment struggled to obtrude themselves; I suppressed the rising sigh; I avoided every object connected with the past; I occupied myself incessantly; I recalled to my thoughts the emphatic counsels and predictions of my deceased patron; I devised means to interrupt and break the chain of habits and associations that was incessantly betraying my resolutions; I remembered the fate denounced for me, even by my tenderest and most indulgent friend, — "To dissolve in dreams of pleasure, to soften in luxurious indolence, belongs not to the destitute orphan, whom *sterner* duties urge to more magnanimous exertions;" I stifled the yearnings of an enervating tenderness, and sought to brace to its highest tone the vigour of my mind. My efforts, strenuous and unremitting, were not wholly fruitless.

Two days previous to that appointed for my departure, as busied, towards the close of evening, in arranging my little household and taking an inventory of my effects, my attention was suddenly arrested by a confused noise in the passage, as of one contending for entrance. An old and faithful servant of my guardian's, who had long served him in various capacities, seemed, in a tone of remonstrance, to be opposing some person who vehemently endeavoured to force his way. The door of the room in which I was employed bursting open, a slight tremor agitated my spirits on beholding Sir Peter Osborne, who suddenly presented himself to my sight. On my rejection of his proposals to my patron, (proposals, which, he conceived, had done me but too much honour,) he had indignantly quitted the country, and resided principally in town, from whence, till this moment, I knew not of his return. Though not absolutely inebriated, he appeared evidently flushed with liquor: his complexion was heightened, while fire seemed to flash from his eyes, as he abruptly accosted me.

"Behold," said he, "the man whose ardent and generous tenderness you repaid with disdain, yet who returns to prove to you his sincerity, to supply to you the friend and protector you have lost. Mr. Raymond, I understand, is no more: whether from negligence or inability, he has, I find with concern, left you in circumstances little suited to your merits or to the delicacy of your sex and education: added to which, the unfortunate events connected with your birth will, I fear, give to your situation peculiar disadvantages. Allow me, then, to be your friend, to recompense you for the injustice of fortune, and to pour into your lap those treasures — "

"And by what authority, sir," impatiently interrupting him, my face crimsoned over with indignation, "do you presume thus to address me? — Though unprotected and destitute, my spirit bends not to my humble fortunes. This house is at present my asylum: your preference is equally unexpected and unwelcome: whatever be my future destination, be assured I will owe no obligation to a man who considers my misfortunes as a privilege to insult me, and who has proved himself alike destitute of humanity and of principle. I insist on your leaving me this moment: I have many affairs of importance to settle during my short stay in the country; nor can I sacrifice my time to an intrusion as impertinent as unseasonable."

Abashed by the courage I assumed, the profligate man of fashion shrunk back hesitating, vainly endeavouring, for some moments, to rally his retreating spirits: his eye sunk under mine, while, stammering, he essayed an incoherent apology.

"Nothing can atone for your behaviour: your late barbarous, unmanly conduct towards my friends has added, to my dislike of your manners and principles, aversion and horror. I will not listen to you; it is with impatience I bear you in my sight: I wanted not this new instance of your callous and inconsiderate nature."

Utterly disconcerted by the vehemence of my manner, after a few moments pause and a visible struggle, he precipitately withdrew.

On the ensuing morning, I received from him a long and contrite letter, (of which I was betrayed into the perusal by a superscription in a feigned hand,) alleging intoxication as an excuse for the abruptness of his behaviour the preceding evening; informing me, that Mr. Pelham, the father of my lover, scrupled not to speak freely among his acquaintance of the calamitous circumstances attending my birth, of the happy escape of his son from my allurements, of the folly and imprudence of my late benefactor in bestowing upon me an education so unfitted to my sex, my situation, and pretensions. To this he subjoined, that Mr. William Pelham had returned, some weeks since, from the continent, where his brother still remained for the entire re-establishment of his health;

that, since his arrival, he had cheerfully acquiesced in a matrimonial engagement, contracted for him, during his absence, by his father, with the rich heiress of a noble family; that, when he left town, the union was on the point of taking place, and was, probably, by this time, completed. He next adverted to, and enlarged upon, my friendless and destitute situation, offering me an ample establishment to undertake the superintendence of his family, concluding with some obscure hints and menaces should his liberal intentions in my favour again suffer a defeat.

The intelligence conveyed to me by this letter affected me with poignant and complicated emotions. William was indeed *lost to me for ever*! was about to become the husband of another! Another would be entitled to those endearments, those caresses, the remembrance of which still melted my heart within me, and dissolved its boasted firmness in a tide of overwhelming softness. I seemed anew compelled to resign him, compelled to abjure the sweet, though latent, hope, which, in despight of reason, and in the face of conviction, had yet lurked within my bosom. Till this moment, I believed that I had renounced him, that I had vanquished my passion, that I was superior to the weakness of sex and nature: deceitful and flattering illusion! that, in the hour of trial, no longer availed me! The pangs of jealousy rent my heart; love, hatred, grief, pride, regret, resentment, despair, by turns assailed it. In the anguish of my soul I abhorred existence, and cursed, in bitterness of spirit, my wretched destiny. Casting my eye once more over the fatal scroll that had torn from my sinking heart its last reed of hope, abhorrence and disdain of the unworthy writer, who thus barbarously insulted my sorrows, revived in my mind, and diverted the tide of passion, while I indignantly tore asunder his humiliating proposals, returning them in a blank cover, without deigning a reply.

On the ensuing morning, stifling in my bosom the anguish which distended it, and suppressing the sighs that struggled to force their way, I resumed the preparations for my departure, discharging the old and faithful domestics of my deceased friend, whose services I was no longer able to reward. We parted with mutual tears and regret, when I took my seat, at an early hour, in a stage-coach,[41] for the metropolis.

Chapter IV

NOTHING WORTHY OF RELATION occurred during my journey, till, at the last stage, as we were about to quit the inn,
a young woman genteelly dressed, with an engaging countenance and a soft insinuating address, came out of an adjoining room, inquiring if she could be accommodated with
a vacant place to town. Being answered in the affirmative,
she lightly stepped into the coach, taking her seat beside
me. During the remainder of the way, she sought, by num-
berless obliging, officious attentions, to attract my regard.
Impressed by the seeming kindness of her manner, my
heart, guileless and unsuspecting, formed for social affections, from which it had been so deplorably cut off, gladly
expanded itself to the delightful sympathies so congenial to
its feelings. As we drew near the place of our destination,
remaining alone with my new companion, our fellow-travel-
lers having alighted, we entered into more frank and familiar conversation. She informed me that she was returning
from the house of a relation, where she had passed some
weeks; that she expected her father's chariot to meet her at
the inn where the coach put up; and that, as I appeared to
be a stranger to the town, she would, with great pleasure,
would I give her leave, set me down at the house of my
friends, if it was not very wide of St. James's Street,[42] in
which she resided, while, by this means, she should gratify
herself, by enjoying, a little longer, the pleasure of my conversation. I hesitated, sighed, and, while I declined her
obliging offer, at length ingenuously confessed my forlorn
and friendless situation, and my uncertainty of the recep-
tion I might meet with in the family to which I was furnished with credentials by my deceased guardian, but to
whom I was personally a stranger. She seemed to be af-

fected by my artless narrative, assuring me, in case of the failure of my present plan, I might depend upon her interest in my favour in the circle of her connections, which was extensive, so much had my appearance and my manners prepossessed her. I expressed, in return, in lively terms, my grateful sense of her kindness.

On our arrival at the inn, we found a plain, but fashionable, chariot in waiting, into which my companion stepped, at the same time giving a commission to her servant to procure for me a hackney-coach,[43] and to assist in removing into it my little baggage. This was quickly accomplished, when I took leave of the obliging stranger with a profusion of acknowledgements, and, having given her my address, received from her an assurance that she would take an early opportunity of calling on me to learn the result of my application. We separated with mutual professions of good will, and I was rapidly conveyed through the tumultuous city, my attention distracted by the novelty and variety of the scene. After passing through several streets and turnings, the coach suddenly stopped before a large and handsome house, at the west end of the town. A servant in livery came to the door to answer my inquiries, by whom I was informed, that the family I named indeed resided there, but were at present from home. He added, observing my perplexity and disappointment, that, would I be pleased to alight and wait their return, I should certainly see them in the course of the evening. Perceiving no other alternative, to this proposal I was compelled to accede. Having alighted, I followed the servant into a spacious drawing-room, where I waited several hours with an anxious, palpitating, heart.

My solicitude increased as the night shut in, and my mind, though I knew not why, for the first time misgave me. Refreshments were, from time to time, officiously offered me by the servants, who passed frequently, on various pretences, with a leering curiosity in their features, in and out of the apartment. In vain I endeavoured to rally my spirits, over which an unconquerable depression stole. The fatigue of my journey, the preceding exhaustion of my mind, the multiplicity of objects that had passed before me, combined to disorder my faculties; a heavy torpor gradually overwhelmed me. I had fallen into a species of rêverie or uneasy slumber when, near midnight, I was roused by a loud and reiterated peal on the knocker of the door. Before I had time to recover from the discomposure occasioned by sounds so novel and alarming, the door of the apartment in which I was sitting being suddenly thrown open, I beheld, with equal terror and surprise, Sir Peter Osborne enter, with an air of easy familiarity, as if master of the house, preceded by a servant bearing additional lights. My powers were for an instant suspended, as I gazed wildly upon an apparition thus terrible and unexpected. The servant having quitted the room, I was accosted by Sir Peter with an air affectedly respectful and deprecating, while he attempted to take my struggling hand.

"What mean you?" said I, half breathless with indignation and astonishment. "Where am I? How came you here? Oh God!" clasping my hands and speaking yet more vehemently, "I doubt, I fear, I am betrayed!"

"Be pacified, my dearest Mary! Do not complain of an innocent artifice that has for its end your benefit, and which nothing but your extreme ignorance of the world, of the perils of your own situation, and your romantic predilection for a man who contemns you, could have rendered necessary. I will freely confess that your perverseness and pride have stimulated me to a stratagem, the occasion for which humbles me. Born to fortune, brought up in indulgence, and accustomed to command, my temper and my wishes ill brook control. When, with lavish fondness, I would have elevated you to a station by which the vanity and ambition of half your sex would have been dazzled, you repaid my liberality with coldness and disdain, and retorted the bitter complaints of disappointed passion with haughty defiance. You may perceive I know not how to court in gentle blandishment, yet still you are the sovereign of my heart: myself, my house, my fortune, are at your command; the study of my life shall be to invent new pleasures — ”

"No more," said I impatiently, endeavouring to rush past him, while he forcibly detained me; "I will not be thus constrained; you have no authority to constrain me; I will go this moment."

"Whither would you go? What madness influences you? — Recollect the time of night, your ignorance of the town. In avoiding fancied evils, the fiction of a romantic imagination, would you rush on certain destruction?"

"I care not! Let me go! I will go; I will not be thus detained!" repeated I, with frantic violence.

He rang the bell, still grasping my hands in his, while I contended vehemently to free myself.

"Tell Catharine to come here," said he, to a servant who appeared at the door. In a few moments, a young woman, gaily, but loosely, dressed, with a pert and bold aspect, entered. "Conduct this lady to the chamber prepared for her," continued he, "and give her every attendance and accommodation which she requires." Then, turning towards me, he entreated me to be calm, swearing solemnly that I should suffer no other inconvenience or injury than a gentle restraint for a few days, to afford him an opportunity of urging those arguments and persuasions, which, he trusted, when I had given them due consideration, would not fail of producing their effect, and of securing our mutual happiness.

I made no reply; but, perceiving farther resistance at present vain, silently followed my conductress, my heart bursting with rage and grief, up another staircase, to a back-chamber elegantly furnished, with a dressing-room adjoining, where, having made a fruitless effort to move the feelings, or tamper with the fidelity, of my attendant, I was left, having refused to accept her services, to my repose. The night was far spent: Catharine, on quitting the chamber, locked the door on the outside, taking with her the key.[44] Opening the shutters, I attempted to raise the sash, but without success; the windows appeared to have been recently fastened down. The moon, which was then near the full, shone brightly, and discovered to me a large paved yard, surrounded by out-houses and stabling. All hope of escape being thus cut off, after bolting my door on the inside, I threw myself, in my clothes, on a sofa in the dressing-room, where, overcome by excessive lassitude, I passed several hours in broken unquiet slumbers.

Eight days elapsed, that afforded to my situation but little variety, on each of which I was persecuted by new importunities and insults. I had hitherto preserved myself from personal indignity; but, while the spirit and courage I laboured to assume appeared to check the audacity of my presumptuous host, I yet perceived, but too evidently, the difficulty with which his haughty impetuous temper submitted to restraint. I had, during this interval, made several ineffectual efforts to liberate myself: worn by anxiety, indignation, grief, and watching, (for, I had taken no other rest since my captivity than short interrupted slumbers on the sofa,) my strength and my fortitude became almost exhausted; a slow fever preyed upon me.

On the ninth day of my confinement, an unusual confusion in the house excited my attention, when I learnt, on inquiry, from Catharine, who was almost my constant companion, that preparations were making for the entertainment of a large company of gentlemen, whom her master had invited to partake of a grand dinner, in compliment to a friend who had but recently returned from a foreign tour. Reflecting upon this intelligence, I determined, if, in the confusion of the day, I should not be able to elude the vigilance of the spies set over my conduct, and effect my escape; to endeavour, on some pretence, to quit my apartments; to force my way into the dining-room, and boldly claim the protection of the company. The more I considered this project the more practicable it appeared to my inexperienced mind.

Hour after hour passed by, while I fruitlessly sought an opportunity of effecting my design. It was near midnight, when, fretted by the tormenting assiduities of my attendant, who had brought into my chamber a variety of dainties, of which she importuned me to partake, and, on my refusal, devoured with greediness, that, pretending sleep, with a view of relieving myself from her incessant volubility, I had the satisfaction of observing her, (parched with thirst from her intemperance, and believing herself unperceived,) from time to time, swallowing copious draughts of Burgundy, from which she presently became completely intoxicated, and fell into a heavy sleep. My heart beat quick, as, with trembling fingers, I drew from her pocket the key of my chamber, and, unlocking the door, with light steps stole slowly down the stair-case.

As I drew near the scene of festivity, the Bacchanalian shouts, the roar of dissolute mirth, bursts of laughter, and boisterous exclamations, suspended my steps, and congealed my blood with terror. My purposes were in an instant blasted; but, the next moment, rallying my spirits, I determined to rush past the dining-room, and make one desperate effort to gain the street. I had proceeded but a few paces, when a confused noise among the guests, as if in motion, obliged me to hasten back precipitately. I had scarcely gained the stair-case, when the door of the dining-parlour flew open, and the company sallied tumultuously forth. As I reached the first landing-place, the sound of footsteps from above, as of several persons descending, cut off my retreat. Distracted and perplexed, I rushed into an open chamber, to conceal myself while they passed, listening in breathless apprehension. Some persons appeared to be talking in the passage: I retreated farther into the room, and gained a small dressing-closet, when, after a few minutes, the sounds that had alarmed me having suddenly ceased, I was about to quit the closet and regain my apartment. At this instant, a light gleamed under the door: hasty footsteps crossed the chamber, and the dreaded voice of Sir Peter Osborne, as speaking to his servant, broke upon my ear. I attempted to shriek; but, overcome with the variety of emotions by which I had been agitated, I uttered only a deep groan, and sunk powerless on the floor; confounded, stunned, as it were, in a state of consternation, that, without depriving me of my faculties, seemed utterly to suspend them. From this unaccountable stupor, this lethargy of the senses, I was roused by the entrance of the vile Osborne. My appearance in his chamber, alike unexpected and extraordinary, — the hour, the solitude, — my defenceless situation, — my confusion, my terror, — my previous exhaustion, — the anxiety and fatigue I had sustained during the past week, — his native impetuosity, heightened by recent scenes of riot and festivity, by surprise, by pride, by resistance, — combined to effect my ruin. Deaf to my remonstrances, to my supplications, — regardless of my tears, my rage, my despair, — his callous heart, his furious and uncontrollable vehemence, — Oh! that I could for ever blot from my remembrance, — oh! that I could conceal from myself, — what, rendered desperate, I no longer care to hide from the world! — I suffered a brutal violation.

*　*　*　*　*　*　*　*

For several succeeding days, a succession of fainting-fits alarmed the wretch to whose barbarous purposes I had fallen a victim, till, at length, after repeated messages and entreaties to be heard, he forced himself into my presence, deprecated my anger, and besought my forgiveness for an outrage, which, he swore vehemently, had not been premeditated, but was the mere result of accident and a temporary effervescence of spirits. Indignation re-animated my desponding mind, and invigorated my frame, as he proceeded to attribute to my severity and scorn the desperate measures into which he had been betrayed, and which, he solemnly assured me, he was far from attempting to justify; yet, since the past could not be recalled, my own good sense and prudence, he trusted, would lead me to attend to and to consider the best means of future reparation.

"O God!" exclaimed I, averting my head impatiently and wringing my hands in indignant agony, "O God, give me patience! — What reparation canst thou, darest thou, to propose? — I demand my liberty this moment; I insist upon being suffered to depart. No one has a right to control me. I will appeal to the tribunal of my country; I will boldly claim the protection of its laws, to which thou art already amenable. — Think not, by feeble restraints, to fetter the body when the mind is determined and free.[45] I ask no mercy; for, bowels of compassion, I know, to my cost, thou hast none; but liberty, the common *right* of a human being[46] to whose charge no offence can be alleged, (yet what rights, cruel violator! hast thou respected?) I once more demand, which to refuse me be at thy peril. I will go. Who dares oppose me?" exclaimed I, attempting to rush past him, stamping with rage, and tearing my hair with anguish, as he struggled to withhold me.

"For heaven's sake! for your own sake! dear, violent, girl!" said the barbarous ruffian, "hear me! I ask only five minutes audience, and I swear by my Maker you shall then go whither-soever you please, and no one shall prevent or oppose you."

"Speak, then; speak quickly; while I have temper, while I have patience, while I have sense, to hear you."

"To whom and where would you go, foolish and unhappy girl? — Let not passion and woman's vengeance blind you to the perils of your situation! — I dare not deceive you; the measures I have been partly driven and partly betrayed into, from which, upon my soul, had I not hoped a better issue, should never have been put in practice, have, I fear, already irretrievably injured your reputation. My servants, I find, have been indiscreet; your romantic lamentations for the consequences of an accident, which a prudent silence might have suppressed, have excited the attention of the house, and the prattling rascals, with the gossips of your own sex, have put their own construction on the chance that threw you into my arms, and have already made us the theme of the neighbourhood. To what purpose, then, these pathetic appeals and unavailing recriminations? What will you do with the freedom for which you so vehemently contend? — Your beauty and unprotected situation may, perhaps, but still farther provoke the lawless attempts of our sex and oppose the sympathy of your own. No one, I doubt, will now receive you in the capacity in which you had proposed to offer yourself, even were it more worthy of you; such are the stupid prejudices of the world. What is called, in your sex, honour and character, can, I fear, never be restored to you; nor will any asseverations or future watchfulness (to adopt the cant of policy and superstition) obliterate the stain. Who will credit the tale you mean to tell? What testimony or witnesses can you produce that will not make against you? Where are your resources to sustain the vexations and delay of a suit of law, which you wildly threaten? Who would support you against my wealth and influence? How would your delicacy shrink from the idea of becoming, in open court, the sport of ribaldry, the theme of obscene jesters?" — I shuddered, groaned, and put my hand to my forehead: my brain seemed on fire. — "Simple girl! how impotent, then, is your rage! how weak your menaces! yet how charming your simplicity! — Be pacified! be wise! Accept my honest contrition and the affluence I offer; reign uncontrolled mistress of my fortune as of my heart."

"Think not, inhuman man, though disgraced in the eye of a misjudging world, think not that I am yet humbled to your purpose. My honour, say you, can never be restored to me? Oh, 'tis false! 'tis base as barbarous! Its lustre, which you have sought to obscure, will break out, in your despight, from the temporary cloud which envelopes it, with undiminished brightness. My spirit, superior to personal injury, rises above the sense of its wrongs, and utterly contemns you! I spurn the wealth you offer, the cursed price of innocence and principle, and will seek, by honest labour, the bread of independence. You have afflicted, but you cannot debase me; my detestation of your odious qualities, though intense, is still inferior to my contempt and scorn: yes, from my very soul, I defy

119

and despise you! The respect of the world, the love of my fellow-beings, once my pride and boast, my incentive to every laudable action, I am content to resign, — if it be indeed true," weeping bitterly, "that, without crime or wilfulness, I must forfeit these envied distinctions. In some obscure retreat, far from the world and its unmerited scorn, unknown, unbeloved, cut off from human sympathy, I will wear out in honest indigence the remnant of my wretched days: I will sink into the grave, solaced only by the approbation of my own heart; a heart, that, till it knew you, knew neither shame nor sorrow."

"Go, then, perverse as obdurate! Go," said the callous Osborne, incensed and mortified, "whithersoever you choose. Try the world, in which you are so bent upon adventuring: your heroic sentiments will, I suspect, prove but a feeble support. When you can descend from these altitudes to common life and feelings, remember that, in me, notwithstanding your violence and obstinacy, you may ever claim a friend."

Saying which, he held open the door, whispering to his servant as I ran, or rather flew, through the passages, panting and breathless, into the street.

Chapter V

IT WAS TOWARDS THE DUSK OF EVENING. I proceeded rapidly on, through many streets and turnings, unconscious to the passing objects, unknowing whither I went, careless of the future, without lodging, without plan or purpose, friendless and unknown, when I was roused from this oblivion of my wants and miseries by a voice that thrilled through my heart, recalling, as by enchantment, my wandering faculties, and awakening me to keen and sudden recollection.

"Mary! Mary Raymond! — Good God! can it be? is it possible?" exclaimed William Pelham, as he snatched my hand, and, with his left arm encircling my waist, supported my fainting steps.

I was in a loose undress, my head uncovered, my long dishevelled hair floating over my shoulders in wild disorder, my looks wan and haggard, my eyes unsettled and frenzied.

"Whence this cruel disorder, this forlorn and terrible appearance? where is your guardian? when did you leave the country? how came you thus? what disaster has befallen you?" were the successive interrogations of Mr. Pelham, to which I attentively listened, without seeming to comprehend either their nature or meaning. An open hotel stood near the spot of our rencontre, into which I passively suffered myself to be led. Retiring to an inner apartment, I sunk half lifeless on a sofa. At the solicitation of my lover, I attempted, but in vain, to swallow a cordial, which, having called for on our entrance, he raised to my parched lips. Perceiving my fruitless efforts, he desisted from importuning me, and, (placing it on a table,) returning, seated himself beside me, sustaining me in his arms,

and resting on his bosom my throbbing head. As in murmurs of tender sympathy he gently soothed me, the perturbation of my spirits gradually subsided. The beloved
accents of a voice associated with so many endearing recollections, so many powerful emotions, lulled every stormy
passion, as by enchantment, to repose. Sheltered in the
arms of William, leaning on his breast, pressed to his
heart, soothed by his tenderness, the painful sense of my
misfortunes, of my wrongs, seemed as on a sudden obliterated. I felt guarded as by a talisman, encompassed in a
magic circle, through which neither danger could assail
nor sorrow pierce me.[47] Absorbed in the present, the past
and the future were, for a period, alike forgotten. My
soul, formed for *love*, felt, in that exquisite moment, its
sensibilities, infinite, exhaustless! — My tears flowed, without effort, in copious streams, soft, balmy, delicious: they
relieved my burning brain and bursting heart: a calmness
like that of smiling infancy stole over my spirits and
hushed them into peace. It was long ere, in reply to the
eager questions of my lover, I could give him a connected,
coherent, reply. I saw him, — I heard him; — I felt his
caresses; — it was enough! my heart rested satisfied! — But
it was not thus with William; he repeated impatiently his
inquiries again and again. I attempted, but in vain, to
satisfy his eager interrogatories: the temporary and deceitful calm I had experienced quickly gave place to convulsive shiverings, that ran along my nerves, while pangs
darted through my temples. I heard the voice of William,
as he continued to speak, as at an immense distance, his
beloved form faded from my sight: unusual sounds rang
in my ears, my thoughts became involved in horror and
confusion, my head seemed a weight which I vainly attempted to raise.

Three weeks that followed were a blank in my existence; yet I had intervals of reflection, dark and dreadful. Imaginary terrors, broken recollections, strange phantoms, wild and wandering thoughts, harassed and persecuted me. In some of these terrible moments, the visionary form of my wretched mother seemed to flit before me. One moment, methought I beheld her in the arms of her seducer, revelling in licentious pleasure; the next, I saw her haggard, intoxicated, self-abandoned, joining in the midnight riot; and, in an instant, as the fantastic scene shifted, covered with blood, accused of murder, shrieking in horrible despair, dragged to the scaffold, sinking beneath the hand of the executioner! Then, all pallid and ghastly, with clasped hands, streaming eyes, and agonizing earnestness, she seemed to urge me to take example from her fate! Her dying groans and reiterated warnings, in low, tremulous accents, continued to vibrate on my ear: they became fainter and fainter, when methought I rushed forward to clasp my hapless parent in a last embrace. I beheld the convulsive pangs, the gaspings, the struggles, the distortions of death. — Starting from these terrific visions, wildly shrieking, my heart palpitating, panting for breath, I sought to recall my wandering reason, while cold dews hung upon my temples, and universal tremblings shook my frame. These visionary terrors subsided by degrees, while the native vigour of my constitution at length gradually triumphed over the shock it had sustained. A heavy, torpid insensibility succeeded to the violence of delirium, from which, after many hours, I recovered, as from a frightful dream, to recollection and sanity.

Mr. Pelham had, with unremitting assiduity, watched every turn of my disorder, and called in to my aid all that medical skill could devise. He continued daily, as I slowly recovered, to visit me, yet methought, amidst the lavish tenderness with which he treated me, I could perceive in his eyes an expression of confusion, reserve, and perplexity. During the succession of calamitous events that had so rapidly succeeded to each other, I had either lost or been robbed of, without the possibility of tracing by what means, the little property bequeathed to me by my guardian. This discovery occasioned me new vexation: I reflected on the pecuniary obligations that, from the expenses attending my illness, I must already have incurred to Mr. Pelham, which, joined with his equivocal, mysterious behaviour, sensibly embarrassed and afflicted me. I determined no longer to defer the explanation of my situation; an explanation which every hour rendered more indispensable, and which my lover hitherto, in consideration as it seemed of my yet unassured health, had, since the first evening of our meeting, forborn to urge.

Having, by every previous effort, sought to nerve my spirits for the occasion, I at length entered with earnestness and solemnity on the cruel detail. I spoke in brief of the events which had succeeded to our separation; of the death of my patron; my purpose in coming to London; the consequences that had ensued; when, betrayed, violated, despoiled I knew not how of my property, without friends or character, without other support than conscious rectitude and a spirit unyielding, I found myself thrown upon the world, a miserable and solitary outcast. I carefully avoided the name of the man to whom I owed my misfortunes, or repeating any circumstance which might lead to the detection: to suffer in the opinion of William was less painful than to endanger his safety. He listened to me with strong and apparent emotion, broke in upon my narrative with bitter imprecations, traversed the room with furious and unequal steps, gnawed his lip as in anguish, struck his forehead, discovering various symptoms of remorse, rage, and anguish.

"It is now," said he vehemently, "that I suffer for my accursed cruelty and folly! It is to me originally that you owe your sufferings! Barbarian, fool, that I was! equally criminal and weak, to sport with the feelings, to contemn the heart, to risk the loss, of such a woman! How can I hope forgiveness for the past? and yet, without it, I feel the future must be intolerable." — He went on to confess, in broken and interrupted language, that, new to the world, its allurements, its pleasures, on his first arrival in Paris, he forgot, in his fascinations, the respect due to himself, to virtue, to the sacred obligations he had voluntarily incurred; that, in a career of dissipation and expense, he had, in the course of his tour, involved himself in embarrassments, which impelled him, on his return, to lend a too compliant ear to the ambitious projects of his father. "Yet think not, my beloved girl," added he passionately, "that your image was ever effaced from my heart! Oh no! in the midst of its wanderings, that dear and lovely image perpetually returned, innocent, affectionate, artless, — returned as in the first days of love and guileless youth, — and, for a moment, compelled me to loathe the follies for which I had lavishly bartered pleasures so ineffably superior. On my arrival in my native country, my first inquiries were after the virtuous and amiable friends of my youth. Of the death of Mr. Raymond, which must have been purposely concealed from me, I knew not till this night. A baronet, a man of fortune, it was rumoured, had made pretensions to the lovely Mary; pretensions, the success of which, I was informed, were universally credited. I felt that, by my own conduct, I had justly forfeited my claims upon her heart. What shall I say? The derangement of my affairs, the importunity of my father, influenced me to examine the advantages of an engagement contracted for me during my absence; an engagement in which I was persuaded the honour of my family was implicated; and I, three weeks since, — became the husband of another!"

He paused: — I started from his arms, in which I had unconsciously suffered him to enfold me: a bolt of ice appeared to shoot through my quivering nerves, succeeded by a burning heat; a convulsive shuddering shook my frame. In the reports of the profligacy and infidelity of my lover, however confirmed by his silence, I had never wholly confided: the convictions which, at one period, I seemed to derive from the information of Sir Peter Osborne, his subsequent baseness had nearly cancelled: (oh, how slow is passion to credit the tale that destroys its hopes!) on this full and fatal confirmation of their truth, a gush of reflections poured impetuously upon my mind; my thoughts darted backward, and, recoiling with rapidity, in the same instant, embraced the future, pointing out, as with a sun-beam, the only part which it now became me to act. Repelling resolutely the emotions that pressed upon my heart, struggling arduously with my feelings, I assumed by degrees an aspect more dignified and composed, when, turning my eye on my companion, I perceived that he attentively marked the changes in my features, while he waited with solicitude till the first tumult of my thoughts had subsided. Observing my cold and indignant glance, he advanced towards me with an air respectful and timid, attempting to retake my resisting hand. Withdrawing it in a manner at once mild and firm,

"Those innocent testimonies of affection," said I, with an assumed resolution, "which indulgent tenderness might yet allow a lover beloved, though wandering, become criminal when yielded to one who has incurred obligations which he cannot violate with impunity, who has given claims to another which honour and duty enjoin him to fulfil."

THE VICTIM OF PREJUDICE

"Hear me, Mary! Drive me not to despair! — Distinguish, I pray you, between the dictates of nature and virtue and the factitious relations of society. By the former, infinitely more dear and sacred, my soul is bound to you, the first and only object of its tenderest sympathy: to the latter I am willing to grant all that can reasonably be demanded, all that was inferred by my engagement. In my nuptials, mutual convenience was the bond of union; affection was, on neither side, either felt or pretended. Let the woman to whom I have given my hand enjoy, with my name and rank, the freedom and privileges sanctioned by the character of a *wife*; let her preside over my family, at my table, in my house; let her be uncontrolled mistress of my fortunes: these are her dues, and for these only is she solicitous: but justice and gratitude alike require that my *affections* should be restored to their dear original possessor, in whose gentle bosom they have long yearned to repose: it is by *her* only that a heart impressed with her image can be reclaimed from its errors."

"Think not, by this sophistry, to seduce my judgement: abandoned to infamy and covered with shame, virtue still maintains her empire in my bosom: *it is virtue only that I love better than William Pelham*; and virtue warns me, in seeking my own gratification, to beware how I plant a thorn in the bosom of another. While uncertain of your engagements, while malice or rumour only whispered the unwelcome tidings, while your own conduct wore a doubtful appearance, while real and visible obstacles opposed themselves not to my trusting heart, while a bare *possibility* nourished hope, a secret consciousness of worth, the credulity, the magic of affection, the sanguine spirit of youth and inexperience, in despight of appearances, of coldness, of neglect, of calamity, of disgrace, of accumulated evidence and increasing difficulty, still sustained me. Jeal-

ousy, accident, absence, misfortune, had no power over a
love like mine; conviction, justice only, could tear it from
my heart. While I shudder at the profligate motives upon
which you have dared to form an union, — an union, that,
disavowed by affection, threatens misery in its most hide-
ous shape, — yet, all destitute and forlorn as are my fortunes, all humbled and degraded my situation, the woman
whose innocence, whose tenderness, whose worth you
contemned, the hopes of whose youth you blasted, whose
maturer years you have consigned to regret, will not, for
the price of present pleasure, barter the principles which,
amidst the wreck of her prospects, now constitute her only
support. — Go! fulfil the obligations you have incurred!
Fulfil your splendid destiny! — Go! be prosperous, be
happy *if you can*! leave me to my fate. With a mind, a
resolution, yet unimpaired, I do not, *indeed I do not*, yield
to despair."

In vain my lover humbled himself before me; in vain
he wept, entreated, remonstrated, urged every argument
which ingenuity, aided by passion, could devise; painted,
in vivid colouring, the evils that beset me; adverted to the
fate of my wretched mother; hinted that society would,
with inexorable malignity, hunt me from its privileges;
that, with a mind peerless and unstained, I should yet
suffer all the penalties of guilt, without possible appeal or
redress; that the consolations of a spotless fame were for
ever denied me; that the prejudices of the world, unrelenting to my sex, would oppose to all my efforts insuperable barriers; that sorrow, contumely, *despair*, would en-
compass me on every side; that toils and snares would
beset my paths and inevitable destruction ultimately overwhelm me.

"Let it come then!" exclaimed I with fervour; "let my
ruin be complete! Disgrace, indigence, contempt, while

unmerited, I dare encounter, but not the censure of my own heart. Dishonour, death itself, is a calamity less insupportable *than self-reproach*. Amidst the destruction of my hopes, the wreck of my fortunes, of my fame, my spirit still triumphs in conscious rectitude; nor would I, intolerable as is the sense of my wrongs and of my griefs, exchange them for all that guilty prosperity could bestow."

"Lovely, unfortunate *enthusiast!*"[48] exclaimed my lover emphatically, while, with folded arms, he gazed tenderly and earnestly in my face, "*thy destiny is indeed severe.*"

The scene became too trying and painful; my exhausted spirits imperiously demanded repose. Complaining of indisposition and fatigue, I prevailed upon Mr. Pelham to leave me, at a late hour, but not till he had forced upon me, for the relief of my present exigences, a ten-pound note, appointing to breakfast with me at an early hour in the morning.

Chapter VI

FAINT AND EXHAUSTED, I retired to my chamber, and threw myself upon the bed, from which, after a short and harassed slumber, I arose, and, demanding pen and paper, addressed myself to Mr. Pelham.

"It is not without anguish," said I, "that I resolve on separating myself from you; it would be temerity to expose myself to a renewal of the preceding evening's conflict. Attempt not to trace my steps; your search would be vain, or productive only of mutual distress. The path to which duty points I am determined to pursue; nothing shall divert my course; neither poverty nor shame can appal me. I will at least have the glory of deserving, though I cannot command, happiness. The money I received from you last night, with a view to my present purpose, to which it was indispensable, the first fruit of my labours shall repay you: for the expense attending my illness, I fear I must be longer your debtor. — *Farewell!* You have taught me, that to confide in the heart of *man* is to lay up stores for sorrow: henceforth I rest on myself.

"MARY."

Having sealed my note and delivered it in charge to a servant, I quitted the hotel at the dawn of day, and wandered to an obscure and distant part of the town in search of apartments fitted to my humble circumstances, where I might conceal myself for a time, while I recruited my strength and spirits. Entering a little shop, invited by a bill pasted on the window, I inquired if, for a few days, I could be accommodated with a lodging; while I shrunk involuntarily from the shrewd features, curious glances, and harsh tones of its mistress, who regarded my appearance with evident suspicion; nor was it till I had repeated my intention of remaining but a short time, and convinced her of my ability to discharge any expense I should incur, that she consented to treat with me.

Having agreed for the hire of a small chamber on the second floor, with clean, but homely, furniture, I took possession of my new apartment with a satisfaction long unfelt: it seemed the first step towards the independence after which my soul had panted. Taking a slight refreshment, I retired to my bed, and, sinking into a long and profound sleep, awoke not until the close of day. I arose refreshed and tranquil: a serene consciousness of duty pervading my bosom stilled its repinings. I looked backward with complacency on a spotless life: the recollection of my misfortunes lost its poignancy when I reflected that by no prudence could they have been averted, nor could any activity have served to repel them. In no one instance had I been wanting to myself, but, passive and helpless, a victim to circumstances over which I had little power.

On the ensuing morning, I prepared myself to attend the lady to whom my deceased guardian had referred me: fortunately I had yet preserved his introductory letter, which I wore about me in a small Morocco case.[49] Ignorant of the town, and dreading to be recognized, I engaged a hackney-coach, and arrived without accident at the place of my destination. After waiting near an hour in an anti-chamber, I was admitted to the presence of the lady. Her aspect was reserved, and her manners cold and stately. She regarded me with scrutinizing attention, and, having run her eye over the contents of the paper which I had presented to her, observed, that her husband, who had formerly, she believed, had a great esteem for my friend, was, at present, out of town and indisposed: on his return, she would consult with him on the subject of my proposals. To which she added some inquiries that

regarded my accomplishments and pretensions; and, re-
marking the date of the letter, demanded the time of my
guardian's decease; where I had since resided; and why,
in conformity to his apparent wishes, my application had
not been earlier.

I felt a crimson glow suffuse my wan cheek, while I
replied, that I had, indeed, come to London immediately
after my irreparable loss, of which I specified the time,
but that various accidents, particularly a severe indisposition, from which I had but recently recovered, had hitherto delayed my purpose.

Observing me for some minutes significantly, she
asked my address, which having presented to her, she
again inquired, with a sagacious and self-important air,
whether that had been my only place of residence since
my arrival in town; to which I answered in the negative;
adding, while I trembled and faultered, that my story was
a melancholy one; that I had, on coming to London, been
betrayed into the house of a profligate man of fortune,
where I had been detained and insulted; that, since my
escape, I had been, for many weeks, confined to my chamber by a violent fever, the consequence of the agitation I
had suffered.

"This is a very extraordinary account," replied she. "In
what part of the town, pray, did this affair happen? and
what was the name of the gentleman against whom you
bring such a singular charge?"

A faint sickness at that moment overspread my heart;
I felt incapable of detailing particulars, at the recollection
of which my very soul recoiled. I answered in brief, that,
to the former part of her question, being a stranger in
London, I was unable to reply: to the latter I entreated
to be excused, as mischief might attend the disclosure.

"Have you sought any redress" resumed she, after a

minute's pause, "for the injuries of which you complain; you have not mentioned their extent, but, from what you seem to imply, they may, possibly, it capable of proof, come under the cognizance of the law."

"Alas, madam! where can an indigent orphan, destitute of friends and counsel, and unacquainted with legal forms, procure redress?"

"And where were you, and how supported, I should be glad to know, during the illness of which you speak?"

I mentioned to her the loss of my property, of which, having been thrown among strangers, I had, no doubt, been robbed; but that accident had led me, in my distress, in the way of a gentleman, formerly a pupil of my guardian's, who had humanely ministered to my necessities, and procured for me that assistance which my deplorable situation required.

"And am I also forbidden to ask the name of this *charitable* gentleman?"

"His name, madam," blushing and hesitating, "is Pelham, the eldest son of the Hon. Mr. Pelham; but I own — I confess — I could wish not to be discovered to him at present."

She fixed her eyes upon my glowing face, and there appeared in them a sarcastic and malicious expression. "Well," continued she, "your story is somewhat strange, to be sure. I expect the return of my husband in a few days, when we will take your case, which, at least, seems to be sufficiently disastrous, into consideration."

I gently and modestly ventured to hint, that my acquirements would, I hoped, enable me to render myself useful; that it was not charity that I presumed to solicit, but an introduction to some reputable employment, by which I might be enabled to support myself, without becoming burdensome to any one.

Gazing upon me with apparent surprise, and with an expression half-insulting, "Upon my word, *young lady*," in an ironical tone of voice, "I meant not to wound your delicacy by an offer of charity; but the accomplishments of which you boast, you will please to recollect, remain yet to be proved, unless, indeed, you rely for your recommendation on the merit of a very pretty face."

An indignant flush of a moment crossed my cheek; but I remembered, that to conform ourselves to our situation, when inevitable, is true wisdom, and the emotion was transient: my reply, modest without servility, appeared to mollify the lady's kindling wrath, whom I quitted, after receiving an assurance of hearing farther from her in the course of the ensuing week.

I employed the interval in making some preparation for the expected change in my circumstances. In my precipitate escape from the house of Sir Peter Osborne, I had left behind me my little wardrobe, which he knew not where to send to me, even had it occurred to him, and of which I dared not attempt the resumption. My hostess, who dealt in linen and other articles of apparel, gave me credit, at an exorbitant price, for what I found immediately requisite; the ten pounds I had received from Mr. Pelham being already nearly exhausted by the expenses of my board and lodging, which, to satisfy the scruples of my hostess, I had paid in advance.

Having completed my little preparations, I waited, with some degree of impatience, the expected summons, when, at the time appointed, a note was put into my hands to the following purport: — That the lady on whom I had waited had made application to the elder Mr. Pelham, with a view of substantiating the truth of my narrative; that her inquiries had proved but little satisfactory, tending to confirm the suspicions my hesitating manner had excited; that Mr. Pelham had heard (by what means it was not important to detail) of my residence at the house of a libertine baronet, the particulars of which were variously reported, and not altogether to my honour; that my *seductions* of his son, who had been some weeks the husband of a lady of family and fortune, were still more evident, and had incensed him to a high degree; that I stood in no relation to Mr. Raymond, though I had assumed his name; that my birth was infamous; that I had been fostered and educated by my patron from motives of charity. These particulars, it was added, were related solely from motives of justice, and in answer to the questions proposed; also to prevent the probable mischiefs which might ensue from the admission of a young woman of such a description into an innocent and respectable family. Some reflections and comments were subjoined by the lady who transmitted to me these cruel calumnies, in a style and manner sufficiently acrimonious.

O God! how terrible were the first indignant feelings that rent my heart on the perusal of this barbarous recital! New to the world, to its injustice, the wrongs I had suffered appeared to me as a dream, the reality of which was wholly inconceivable. I penetrated not, at the instant, into the extent of the evil to which I felt myself a helpless, devoted victim. Panting, half-breathless with emotion, I flew to justify my fame. Unmindful of decorum, I hurried through the streets with a disordered pace, rushed into the house, and had, without question or ceremony, proceeded half-way up the stair-case, towards the dressing-room in which I had before been admitted to audience, when I found myself forcibly arrested and pulled back.

"My lady," said a man-servant in a gay livery, who had followed me unobserved, "is not at leisure to receive company."

"For God's sake!" I exclaimed in a frantic tone, wringing my hands in impatient agony, "for God's sake, my good friend, lead me to your mistress!"

"My mistress," repeated the fellow pertinaciously, with airs of office, "will see no one at present; she is going out of town to my master, who is dangerously ill, and she will not be broken in upon."

"Have pity," involuntarily sinking on my knees, "oh, have pity upon a poor young creature, betrayed, calumniated, ruined!"

Unable to say more, my tottering limbs failed me; a mist overspread my eyes; while, overpowered by the passions that crowded tumultuously upon my heart, I sunk into a swoon, and should have fallen to the bottom of the stairs but for the support of the servant with whom I had been contending. On recovering my senses, I found myself in the hall, surrounded by the domestics, of whom some sneered and tittered, while others appeared to compassionate my evident distress. Perceiving my hope of being admitted to their lady at present fruitless, I requested pen and paper, and, in a short address, implored, in the sacred names of justice and humanity, only to be permitted to make my defence; adding, that I would call the ensuing day, at the same hour, for that purpose. Having folded, sealed, and given my paper to a young woman, who appeared to regard me with a degree of sympathy, and who engaged faithfully to deliver it to her mistress, I returned to my apartment, my spirits sunk in a fearful despondency.

It was now that I felt all the horror of my destiny. "O wretched and ill-fated mother!" I exclaimed, in the bitterness of my soul, while I wrung my hands with frenzied anguish, "what calamities has thy frailty entailed upon thy miserable offspring! Would to God thou hadst never given me existence! Would to God thou hadst strangled me at my birth!" — Daughters of levity, reflect ere you give the reins to voluptuousness, reflect on the consequences in which ye are about to involve your innocent, devoted, offspring!

Early the next morning, I received a verbal message, by the young woman who had taken charge of my note, importing, that Mrs. — had, a few hours before, left town; that it was not possible for her to doubt that the principal facts alleged against me were true, and, as they afforded ample reason against my admittance into her family, she was not solicitous respecting the particulars; that she had no inclination to expose herself to my vehemence; and that she was gone into the country to join her husband, whence her return was uncertain.

This new instance of injustice operated rather to mitigate than to increase my distress; I became familiarized, as it were, to suffering: exhausted nature refused to supply the sources of grief, a torpor stole over my feelings, I submitted to undeserved injury with sullen resignation, while my spirit, conscious of its purity, rose with dignity superior to its woes.

Chapter VII

THE TEN POUNDS I had received from Mr. Pelham, which had been appropriated to my immediate and imperious wants, had, for some time, been exhausted. The sense of obligation, where I was compelled to withdraw my esteem, pressed heavily on my mind; added to which, I had incurred a small debt to my hostess. As the tumult of passion subsided, I revolved in my thoughts various plans for the support of a comfortless existence. Among the recreations of my youth, connected with my botanical studies, had been the art of drawing and colouring plants and flowers, in the performance of which, directed by my patron, I had acquired taste and facility: it was probable, I sought to persuade myself, that I might convert what had been once my recreation into a more important resource. I sallied out, in the hope of realizing this flattering suggestion.

Without recommendation or introduction, my first day's research was productive only of cold negatives and discouraging objections. Wounded, but not despairing, on the second morning my hopes revived, when the master of a print-shop of a shewy appearance, after attentively considering me for some moments, and putting various questions to me respecting my skill and practice, agreed to make trial of my ability and dispatch. I returned with my patterns to my humble lodging, with light spirits and a beating heart, anticipating the dignity of INDE-PENDENCE. Stimulated by motives thus powerful, I surpassed the expectation of my employer; a new creation, blooming and vivid, rose beneath my pencil: abandoning the models, and disdaining control, my fancy wantoned in luxurious varieties; every new effort brought an access of profit and of praise. I returned, with the produce of my labours, in a blank cover, the ten pounds to Mr. Pelham, and paid off a part of my debt to my hostess.

My heart, for a time, while occupied by this pursuit, forgot, with its griefs, its social propensities, and I began to taste repose, till, one morning, coming out of the house of my employer, I encountered on the threshold a man who peered impertinently under my hat, and in whose features I recollected, with terror, a favourite valet of Sir Peter Osborne's. I attempted, but it was too late, to conceal myself from him: I perceived he knew me; while, hurrying to my lodging, and turning my head on my entrance, I had the additional vexation of observing him, at a little distance, watching my steps. It was some hours before I recovered from the shock of occasioned by this incident, but I at length began to persuade myself that my alarm was groundless; that it was not likely, after so long a period had elapsed, and after what I had already suffered, that any new machinations would be formed against me.

At the expiration of three days, having completed my allotted task, and having been more than ordinarily attentive to the finishing touches of a beautiful pair of firescreens, I carried home my work rather later than usual. My employer, from commending my taste and ingenuity in exaggerated expressions, suddenly seized my hand, and, pressing it gently, at the same time leering in my face and tapping my glowing cheek, made an abrupt transition from the merit of my performance to the charms of my person, on which he expatiated in terms still warmer and more extravagant. I shrunk from his touch with a mixed sensation of terror and disgust, and, turning from his ardent gaze, abruptly withdrew my hand from his.

"What is the matter with my charming girl?" said he, in a voice odiously whining and affected.

Overcome by the recollections which crowded upon

my mind, I was unable to reply; while, folding his arms round me, and muttering words of tenderness in low and half-suppressed tones, he insidiously drew me towards him. Indignation restored my faculties; I broke from him, and burst into a flood of tears.

"My dear little angel," said the insulting wretch, "why this distress? why these pretty romantic airs? Sir Peter Osborne and Mr. Pelham found less difficulty, I have a notion, with my charmer. It is time you abated a little of this theatrical coyness."

Disengaging myself from his grasp, and rushing from the room, I flew through the shop, and gained the street. The precipitation of my escape did not, however, save me from hearing, as I passed, the ribaldry and cruel comments of the young men employed in the business, by whom, in my flight, I was compelled to pass. Regaining my apartment in an agony of passion, I perceived that the fatal tale of my disgrace pursued and blasted all my efforts, when, throwing myself on my bed, I gave way to a burst of grief. Having vented my anguish in a flood of tears, a profound sleep gradually stole over my perturbed spirits, from which I awoke not till towards morning, when I felt myself refreshed and calmed. My first thought, on a recollection of the preceding evening's transaction, was, to change my abode and name, (that of Raymond, which I had for a time thoughtlessly assumed, or rather habitually suffered, and to which I had no claim, I had, since the cruel charge of Mr. Pelham, exchanged for the name of my unfortunate mother;) but this suggestion I presently resisted. — "I am guiltless," I repeated to myself; "why should I then affect disguise, or have recourse to falsehood? In every honest and consistent means of safety I will not desert myself. It is not necessary that I should wilfully spread the tale of my own disgrace or imprudence,

yet I will not, by prevarication, shrink from their consequences." — Neither was it practicable immediately to quit
my lodging; for, in repaying my debt to Mr. Pelham, and
defraying the expenses of a scanty subsistence, I had ex-
pended my little profits; and, for the remainder of the
sum due to my hostess, I was still in arrears. For the drawings carried home the preceding evening I was yet unpaid;
but, in claiming my right, I might possibly subject myself
to new insult. I shuddered, and turned with horror from
the idea; nor dared I employ an agent in my behalf. To
demand my dues would be but to revive and propagate
the tale of my shame.

I revolved in my mind, selected, and rejected, as new
obstacles occurred to me, a variety of plans. Difficulties
almost insuperable, difficulties peculiar to my sex, my age,
and my unfortunate situation, opposed themselves to my
efforts on every side. I sought only the bare means of
subsistence: amidst the luxuriant and the opulent, who
surrounded me, I put in no claims either for happiness,
for gratification, or even for the common comforts of life:
yet, surely, *I had a right to exist!* — For what crime was I
driven from society? I seemed to myself like an animal
entangled in the toils of the hunter. My bosom swelled
with honest indignant pride: I determined to live; I determined that the devices of my persecutors should not overwhelm me: my spirit roused itself to defeat their malice
and baffle their barbarous schemes. From the deplorable
circumstances in which I felt myself involved, I seemed
but to acquire new strength and courage: I exerted my
invention, and called every power into action.

On the first floor of the house in which I occupied
an apartment resided an engraver, to whom I applied to
instruct me in the principles of his art, in which, I conceived, my skill in drawing and knowledge of the science

of proportions might give me facility. He coldly answered, that, for a certain pecuniary gratuity, (which, alas! I was utterly unable to procure,) customary in the profession, he was willing to accept my services, and afford me the necessary assistance. Thus baffled, I once more, with patient, but determined, perseverance, issued forth in search of occupation. To my application, in various shops and warehouses, for embroidery, child-bed linen, useful or fancy work, I was required to bring sureties for my character, or to leave the value of the goods entrusted to me: either of which were, in my circumstances, alike impracticable. I solicited at the music-shops to be permitted to copy notes, but in vain, they had already more applications than they were able to comply with, and a general prejudice seemed to be entertained against my sex and my dejected appearance.

I returned to my lodging wearied and dispirited, when, for the first time, I ventured to request the recommendation of my hostess, if, in the circle of her acquaintance, she could procure me employment. She surveyed me with a suspicious and scowling air, complained of the inconvenience she suffered from my tardy payments, and gave but little encouragement to my proposition.

What was now to be done? I had not tasted nourishment through the day; my resources appeared to be at an end; my finances were at the lowest ebb, nor could I devise any method of recruiting them; a few hours, and, perhaps, perishing with famine, I should vainly seek a shelter for my defenceless head! The most deplorable destitution menaced me. One only project at length occurred, — *servitude*. I shivered, sighed! A faint glow tinged, for a moment, my faded cheek, while a tear forced its way! I now renewed my inquiries, and sought to procure myself admittance, in a domestic capacity, (I cared not in what department,) in some reputable family. Three days wore away in fruitless research: for one place, I was too young and inexperienced; for another, too genteel and pretty; at a third, my hands were objected to, as apparently unaccustomed to labour, and my whole appearance as too delicate and sickly; at others, a recommendation and character were required from my previous place of residence, while coarse conjectures were hazarded on my inability to satisfy these demands. At length, I received casual information that a lady, about to travel, wished to be accompanied by a young woman well educated, possessing acquirements superior to common pretensions, who would have no objection to an absence of some years from her native country. I eagerly listened to a proposal so suited to my forlorn circumstances, and immediately repaired to the apartments of the lady, by whom I was received with civility and kindness; while, expressing herself pleased with my appearance and manner, and observing my apparent fatigue and dejection, she invited me to rest myself and to take some refreshment. To the common sympathies of social and polished life, I had been of late so little accustomed, that, affected by these humane attentions, I snatched involuntarily the hand of my promised benefactress, and burst into a passionate flood of tears. She appeared concerned at this sudden emotion and interested by my distress; and, on my informing her that I was an unfortunate orphan, with no one to aid or recommend me, professed herself inclined to wave, in my favour, (so much had my grief and artless behaviour impressed her,) the customary precautions on these occasions. She purposed leaving England, she informed me, the beginning of the ensuing week, when (if, on inquiry, the person with whom I lodged appeared to bear a good character, and would vouch for my conduct since my residence with her)

she would immediately receive me, without farther research, into her service and protection. The kindness of
this amiable woman won all my confidence: I was about
to throw myself at her feet, and narrate, with simplicity,
the disastrous events of my past life, when the entrance
of some persons on business, preparatory to her intended
tour, engaged her attention, and suspended, for the present, my purpose. I withdrew myself, expressing a fervent
and grateful sense of her goodness, and, returning to my
apartment full of hope, my mind relieved from an intolerable pressure, related to my hostess what had passed,
engaging, if, by her means, I could happily procure a situation so desirable, to purchase from her a few more articles indispensable to my approaching expedition, and, on
the day previous to my quitting her, to give her a letter
of recommendation to a gentleman of rank and fortune,
who would, I was assured, gladly reimburse her for the
money she had advanced.

Every thing appeared to succeed to my wish. the day
of my embarkation was appointed by a message from my
patroness; on the evening preceding which, I was to join
her at her apartments. I saw her once or twice during the
interval, but always in the hurry of preparation. In the
morning of a day joyfully anticipated, a day which was to
bear me far from the persecutions that had unrelentingly
pursued me, from a country that had cast me out like an
alien from its bosom, I addressed a few lines to Mr. William Pelham, briefly stating my late distresses and necessities, requesting him to satisfy the demand of the bearer,
with whom I had been compelled, by imperious necessity,
to contract a debt of twenty pounds; adding, my repug-
nance to adopt a mean to which unprecedented persecutions and calamities had driven me; a mean, to which,
while remaining in the same country, no consideration

could have induced me; and expressing my resolution, should future fortune empower me, to repay, with interest, this last testimony which I should ever exact of his former friendship.

Having sealed and superscribed this paper, I was proceeding, not without a painful and revolting feeling, to deliver it to my hostess, previous to my intended departure from her house, when, abruptly bursting into my chamber, she put into my hands a small parcel, which I opened with trepidation. Its contents were five guineas and a letter, from the lady under whose protection I was about to place myself; stating, that a man of fashion and fortune, an acquaintance of her husband's, with whom he had spent the preceding evening, had informed him (my name having been accidentally mentioned as a young person engaged to go abroad with his family) of some particulars, respecting the former incidents of my life and conduct, that had occasioned her the sincerest concern, but, at the same time, had rendered my residence with her somewhat improper; that the gentleman had assured them my present distress was, in a great degree, wilful; that I had kind friends, who could I be prevailed upon to return to them, would, he was assured, gladly receive me; that he expressed himself with seeming frankness, and was apparently well acquainted either with me or my family. Some circumstances, she subjoined, had hastened their departure from London a day earlier than they had purposed; that, had she continued in England, she should have felt much inclined to have investigated farther this affair; nevertheless, that she would ingenuously tell me that such imputations, of which circumstantial evidence was given, must, from various motives, have precluded my admittance into her family; yet, had she found me either traduced or reclaimable, she would have been my friend;

at present, she must satisfy herself with requesting my acceptance of the five guineas enclosed, to preserve me from the pressure of immediate necessity. She concluded with prudent counsel, expressions of regret, and kind wishes; adding, that, by the time her letter reached my hand, she should be advanced on her journey towards the southern coast, the travelling-carriage, at the period of her writing, being in waiting.

Stunned by this unexpected event, I remained during some minutes motionless, my limbs unnerved, my faculties locked up in a deadly stupor, from which the importunate clamours of my hostess at length roused me, who, having acquainted herself with the contents of the fatal mandate that had fallen from my hand, reiterated loudly her demands for the promised letter, by which the payment of her debt was to be assured. Placing my hand on my breast, I drew from the bottom of my heart a heavy sigh, and, the next instant, broke into a convulsive peal of laughter; while confused, but vivid, images danced before my dazzled sight. Making a strenuous effort to regain my wavering faculties, I suddenly caught, (led by the eager eye of my hostess,) from a small escritoir, on which, on her entrance, I had thrown it, the paper recently addressed to Mr. Pelham, and, tearing it in a thousand fragments, scattered them on the floor.

The meaning of this action escaped not the penetrating eye of my sagacious creditor, who, after pouring forth a torrent of invective, and overwhelming me with opprobrious epithets, darted out of the room, threatening me, at her departure, with a vengeance which, at the instant, I did but obscurely comprehend. Seating myself at the feet of my humble pallet, I waited the execution of her menaces with the calm resignation of despair.

Chapter VIII

NEAR TWO HOURS ELAPSED, when, followed by a stranger, from whose ferocious aspect, rugged features, and lowering brow, I involuntarily recoiled, my hostess re-entered.

"I arrest you," said her companion, laying his hand on my shoulder, while I shrunk appalled from his rude grasp, "at the suit of this good woman, to whom you are indebted, for board, lodging, and sundry articles of wearing-apparel, the sum of twenty pounds."

"Lead on," said I, with assumed firmness. "I resign myself to my destiny."

My conductor stopped at the door of the apartment, and held, for a few minutes, a whispering conversation with my creditor, to which she nodded complacently, as in assent. A hackney-coach waited, into which I threw myself, followed by my companion. In profound silence, we passed through various streets and lanes; at length stopping in an obscure part of the town, before a house large and gloomy, the windows defended by bars of iron. Assisted by my guide, I alighted, following him through long and dark passages, up a narrow stair-case, into a small back-room wretchedly furnished, the windows of which, obscured by dirt, shed, as the twilight shut in, a glimmering, uncertain light, according with the melancholy desolation of the place. Sinking into an old-fashioned arm-chair, worm-eaten and tottering, I resigned myself to reflections, that succeeded each other in long and mournful trains. I beheld no person but my conductor, who, for some time, officiously busied himself in arranging the scanty furniture, and presently abruptly addressed me.

"This is not, I confess, a very suitable place for so pretty a lass, but it will be your own fault if you remain here long."

"What mean you, man? Does your office authorize you to insult your prisoners?"

"This is not a prison, pretty maid, nor am I a gaoler."

"What then?" (half-breathless with undefined terror;) "and who are you?"

"A sheriff's officer, who have, from courtesy, brought you to my own house,[50] whence, if you will be persuaded to procure bail, you may depart whenever you please."

"I have no one to bail me; I have neither property nor friends; I am wholly unable to satisfy you for your accommodations, and, therefore, for your own sake, you will do well to remove me without farther delay."

The fellow muttered some things half-inwardly, in which I could distinguish the phrases "d—ned pride" and "artful little b—ch." "Well, well," resumed he, "there's a fine gentleman who is willing, if you will not jilt him again, to pay your debts, and to save you from rotting in gaol."

Springing from my feet in a frenzy of terror, I rushed towards the door, when it suddenly flew open. A person entered bringing lights, and preceding my old and barbarous enemy, Sir Peter Osborne. Uttering a fearful shriek, I fell in convulsions at his feet.

It was long before I returned to recollection, when I found myself stretched on a wretched mattress, attended by several women, who were busily occupied in effecting my restoration. My eyes, wildly turning, sought, on every side, the terrific vision that had appeared as the chimera of a distempered brain, and before which life and sense had fled. I uttered a thousand incoherent interrogations, to which no answer was returned. Dashing from me the cordials with which they continued to importune me, I rose from the bed, and, throwing myself on my knees in a distant part of the room, covered my face with my handkerchief, reclining it on my folded arms, which rested on a window-seat. The footsteps of a man treading softly across the floor caught my attention: starting on my feet, I turned, when the bailiff approached, followed by his guest. Indignation strung my enfeebled nerves: advancing, with hasty steps, towards the master of this miserable abode, I seized his arm.

"If," said I, "you are indeed what you pretend to be, and not the agent of this base man, do your office, and that quickly. I demand the prison you threaten: I will owe no obligations to a wretch whose presence blasts my sight. It is no less your duty to preserve me from insult than from escape: you are amenable to the laws by which I suffer, and, by the peril of those laws, I adjure you, this instant, to lead me hence, and conduct me to the place of my destination.

The fellow stared, appeared half-confounded, and gave back a few paces. The barbarous Osborne, passing him, advanced, and, throwing himself at my feet, with feigned passion, snatched my hand, attempting to press it to his lips. Springing from his touch, and rushing past the officer, I once more endeavoured to gain the door, but discovered it, with inexpressible anguish, to be locked. Staggering towards a chair, and supporting myself on the back, an agony resembling the pangs of death shook my frame.

"Dear, unaccountable creature!" exclaimed the wretch who thus pursued me to my destruction, "what is it that thus alarms and disturbs you? In the presence of this honest man, I ask but one quarter of an hour's conference. You are in the hands of a king's officer; I have no power over you. Hear me but patiently, and may God for ever blast me, if I cannot prevail upon you to listen to reason, and to permit me to liberate you, if I do not that instant depart, and leave, if you will have it so, the law to take its course; nor will I any more molest you by the presence of a man who adores you, who is solicitous only to repair the wrongs into which his passion has hurried him, yet against whom you entertain prejudices so unreasonable!"

I attended in speechless anguish, my hands and eyes raised to heaven. He went on to recapitulate, and to place in their strongest light the horrors of my situation: lost to fame, to hope, to the possibility of salvation; abandoned to all the accumulated evils of indigence and infamy! — "What is this bugbear virtue," continued he, "at the barbarous shrine of which you offer up all the lavish gifts of nature and fortune? — Was that beauteous frame formed to endure the squalid miseries of famine and destitution? to mix in the loathsome gaol with the refuse of mankind? to herd with robbers, prostitutes, and felons? to perish with want, with contagion, with consuming grief, or devouring anguish? On one side, shame, despair, death, await you; on the other, lavish fortune, sheltering love, gaiety, pleasure, adulation, an adoring lover, an admiring world. — The guilt of which you accuse me, I repeat, was but the proof of frenzied passion, driven by your scorn to despair and outrage. Refuse not the reparation which a penitent heart yearns to bestow: a legal settlement, liberal beyond your hopes or your ambition, shall secure to you, in future, the independence, the affluence, the splendour, which charms like your's are fitted to adorn."

"No, no, no! no more, no more!" said I, in a tone of impatient agony, wringing my clasped hands. "Profane not with unhallowed lips the sacred name of LOVE! Oh! how incapable is thy sordid soul of conceiving its generous sentiments, its exquisite sensibilities! Base, selfish, inhuman, barbarian, to see thee is misery, to listen to thee intolerable anguish! — Welcome, welcome," continued I, my hands spread, my cheeks glowing, my eyes lighted with a transient lustre, "desolation, infamy, a prison, the rack, death itself! All, all is light, is balmy, compared with the misery of thy detested presence, — *cruellest of men!* — on whom may the curses of the orphan and destitute fall!"

"Once more, then, stubborn beauty, I abandon you to your fate. And yet, — and yet, — " continued he, approaching me.

"Begone! this instant begone! Advance not! — Dare you," repeated I, with frantic vehemence, my senses disturbed with terror, "dare you, betrayer, spoiler, thus insidiously approach? — Man," seizing once more the arm of the officer, "on thy peril, protect me, as thou wouldst answer it at a higher tribunal!"

Alarmed by the energy and violence of my manner, my enemy at length suffered himself to be prevailed upon, by the rude eloquence of the bailiff, who began to be apprehensive for the credit of his house, to retire; but not till he had pressed me to permit him, unconditionally, to discharge the debt for which I had been committed, and to free me from my present restraint. I rejected his offer with firmness and disdain, determining to submit to any evil rather than be indebted to the liberality of a man whom I regarded, with horror, as the cause of my unmerited sufferings. As he descended the stairs, "A *prison*," said he, in an affected, but audible, whisper, to the fellow who accompanied him, "may yet bring her to reason, conquer this obstinacy, and banish her romantic whims. Let the law, then, *for the present*," lowering his voice, "take its course."

Overwhelmed by lassitude, and worn out with fatigue,

after barricading every avenue to the chamber, which was also fastened on the outside, I sunk on a couch, and obtained, the night being far advanced, a few hours of restless and interrupted slumber.

Chapter IX

SOON AFTER THE DAWN of day, I was roused by a summons to prepare for my departure. Again I followed the officer into a carriage prepared for me, and was conveyed to the gloomy gates of a prison. A transient shuddering chilled my blood as the massy doors opened on their hinges. I had proceeded but a few paces, through a winding passage, when a confused sound of voices assailed my ear: methought I distinguished tones not unfamiliar to me, when two men approached, seemingly in earnest conversation. Grey locks shaded the temples and waved over the shoulders of him who appeared to be the elder, and whose voice had excited my curiosity; while his face was partly turned from me. We were obliged to pass each other, the strangers apparently coming from the interior of the prison. Examining intently, as they drew near, the venerable aspect of him, the tones of whose voice had awakened my attention, he suddenly turned and met my earnest gaze, when, O God! what were my emotions on beholding the late faithful domestic of my deceased patron! he, whose feeble arm had, on the evening previous to my fatal journey, vainly attempted to repress the audacity of our powerful neighbour. "*James!*" said I, with emphasis, in a heart-thrilling accent, that partook of all the mingled sensations of my agonized soul. He leaped some paces backward, placed his hand on his breast, and, in a moment, returning, examined my features with wild and eager curiosity.

"God bless my soul!" exclaimed the honest creature, after a short pause; "is it possible? can it be my sweet young mistress, — so pale, so altered, so woe-begone? — In a prison, too! — Oh! had my good old master lived to see his darling thus, his kind heart would have burst asunder."

"Yes, James, you indeed see me wretched, but not guilty; my innocence and my integrity still remain to me."

"Well, blessed be God for that! — London, I am told, is a sad, wicked place, and, meeting you here in this pitiful plight, I knew not what to think; but your kind voice and sweet face (though I must say it is woefully changed) assure me that you are still the same dear, good, young creature I ever knew you. — But — but — I hope," his accents faultering, "that you are not obliged to *remain* in this terrible place. What crime can you have committed, poor innocent lamb! that can deserve a prison?"

"The crime, James, of owing twenty pounds for food and lodging. — Robbed of the little property bequeathed to me by our beloved patron, unable to procure honest employment, compelled to support a wretched being, I was obliged to incur a debt which I am utterly incapable of repaying."

The officer here roughly interposed. "If you can bail the young woman, say so at once; but do not make me stand here, and waste my time, listening to idle prate. Had she not been wilful and stubborn, she had no need to be here; but now the law must and shall have its course."

"But the *law*," replied the good old man, "the barbarous law shall not have my kind old master's darling for twenty pounds. Tell me what I must do, and I will be bound for the debt."

"*You!*" replied the fellow sneeringly. "What security have you to give?"

"Ah! leave me, dear, kind old man, leave me to my fate! I cannot accept the reward of your honest toil. My heart is sinking; my woes, I feel, will not be long."

"But your dear heart shall not sink, and you shall yet live to see many, many happy days, when my grey hairs are laid in the dust. The little property which I have was the gift of my generous master, who overpaid my services: it gladdens my old heart that it should enable me to save his darling child. What better use could I ever put it to? I am yet heart-whole and able to labour, and will work for my dear young mistress, who is worth a hundred such old fellows as I am."

I melted into tears of grateful tenderness: any farther opposition, I perceived, would be fruitless. The sanguine ardour of my temper once more revived; I believed I might, in future, by persevering industry, triumph over my malignant fortune, and reward the beneficence of this faithful domestic. Yielding to his importunities, I suffered him to liberate me, his friend joining in the security, and retired with him to a decent, but humble, lodging.

The good old man was, on our way, all rapture and exultation. The transport of his heart ran over in innumerable affectionate loquacities, every instant entreating pardon for his freedom.

"Pain me not, my friend," said I, "by these unnecessary humiliations: from any other they would seem, in my forlorn circumstances, mockery; from you, they distress me. Are we not equals; or, rather, are you not my deliverer and benefactor?"

"No, no, dear lady! you must still suffer me to be your affectionate servant. I have paid you back but a very small part of the debt I owed my good master."

After the departure of his friend, I related briefly to this humane creature the narrative of my sufferings. — During the recital, his countenance reflected, as in a mirror, the varied feelings which penetrated his heart. He interrupted me incessantly with bitter imprecations on the destroyer of my repose.

"O the barbarous ruffian!" exclaimed he vehemently,

his hands clenched, and stamping on the floor. — "Oh! that my feeble arm could reach his cruel, treacherous heart! — Could I have believed that the sweet infant I had so often dandled in my arms, the lovely child on which my good master so fondly doated, would have been exposed to suffer wrongs like these, never, never would I have been persuaded to quit her. — D—n him! d—n him! (God, forgive me!) a cruel villain!" —

"Stop, my good friend; curse not. Thank heaven it is I who am the *injured*, not the *injurer*. Reflections on the past are fruitless as painful: let us rather look forward; my mind, unviolated, exults in its purity; my spirit, uncorrupted, experiences, in conscious rectitude, a sweet compensation for its unmerited sufferings. The noble mind, superior to accident, is serene amidst the wreck of fortune and of fame. No, pure spirit of the best of men!" clasping my hands and raising my eyes, while a divine fire pervaded my frame, "I will not disgrace thy precepts, I will not desert myself, though I perish in the toils that entangle my steps! I will at least die with the consolation of having deserved the recompense that has hitherto eluded my eager grasp."

James wept like an infant, and audibly sobbed. "Dear, blessed lady!" said he, in a voice half-choked with emotion, "you are, you are, — indeed, — the true daughter of my worthy master! — Accursed be the wretch! May lightnings blast — "

I turned to him an eye of mingled kindness and reproof: he felt its meaning, and, covering his venerable forehead with his clasped hands, continued to weep in silence. To divert the tide of passion which seemed to overwhelm him, I inquired to what fortunate circumstance I owed our meeting and my consequent liberation, when all human aid appeared to have forsaken me. In answer to which he informed me, that he had travelled to London for the purpose of selling out of the funds the sum of fifty pounds, the savings of his labour, assisted by his late master's liberality. With this money he was to enter upon a small farm, which he had undertaken to occupy and rent, on Sir Peter Osborne's manor. That the business had already been transacted, and the agreement signed, between him and Sir Peter's steward, otherwise, he swore vehemently, he would have had no concerns with such a villain. That, not having been in town for many years, he had, with a friend, visited the various edifices and curiosities of London, and had, that morning, been prevailed upon to accompany him on an errand of beneficence to the prison, where, on their return, they had fortunately encountered me. That he knew me not, such ravages had distress made upon my features, till the accent in which I pronounced his name struck at once upon his heart. — I interrupted the overflowings of that kind heart by reminding him that the money he had advanced for my release would, I had but too much reason to fear, incapacitate him for fulfilling his engagements with the steward.

"True," said he, looking somewhat thoughtful and perplexed, as if the idea had not before occurred to him; "but Mr. Steward will, I hope, give me time. Frugality and industry, with a fair harvest, may set all matters right again, and I cannot now want a motive to bestir myself."

It was so long since I had experienced the greetings of cordial friendship, or listened to the tones of sympathy, that I tasted, in the honest affection of this humble creature, a sweet and ineffable consolation. We consulted together on the means which it would be proper to adopt for our future conduct.

I seemed hitherto to have been surrounded by invis-

THE VICTIM OF PREJUDICE

ible agents and hidden snares, that had blasted my purposes, beset my paths, and frustrated my most sagacious plans; yet, intrepid in innocence, I determined to assume no disguise, neither to leave unessayed any upright methods or vigorous efforts to defeat the malice of my adversaries. Disgusted with the train of misfortunes that had, with unmitigable severity, pursued me since my residence in town, I resolved on returning to the scenes of my childhood, and seeking in rural shades a shelter from my pitiless foes.

At the entreaty of honest James, whom thenceforth I determined to cherish with filial care, I consented to accompany him to his farm, (that was happily situated on the extreme verge of the manor, several miles distant from the mansion-house,) the internal concerns of which I undertook to manage, with the business of the dairy, in which I had, for my amusement, and to gratify my patron, acquired some skill in the happy period of my youth.

Chapter X

WE QUITTED LONDON; and, in a few days, were in possession of our little farm, the steward having accepted from my
benefactor a bond for the deficient twenty pounds. We entered upon our rural occupations with alacrity. The intervals
of my domestic employments, in which I acquitted myself
with dexterity and diligence, were devoted to the acquisition
of knowledge, with what scanty materials I was able to procure in this sequestered situation. The school-master of the
village assisted me with some books; I resumed my botanical
studies, which afforded me an object for my walks and for
my pencil; I exercised my affections by occasional instructions to the children of the peasants, and by administering
to the wants and infirmities of our sick and aged neighbours; while, in the evening, it was my delight to solace the
fatigues of my kind friend after the labours of the day.

Six months elapsed in occupation and tranquillity. It
was now that I began to taste the sweets of independence,
the dignity of an active, useful life. Conveniences multiplied in our neat and pleasant abode: without superfluity,
we enjoyed a temperate plenty, and even, by frugality and
self-denial, the exalted pleasure of beneficence. Beloved
and respected by our neighbours, my heart once more
expanded itself to sympathy, my cheeks recovered their
bloom, my eyes their spirit and lustre. I began to persuade
myself that the malice of my fortune was exhausted; that
I should, at length, reap the harvest of my activity and
perseverance. I redoubled my cares and tenderness to my
benefactor, whom I considered not merely as the saviour
of my life, but as the instrument of all that rendered that
life dear and respectable. But in the midst of these flattering prospects a storm was gathering; the clouds began

to lower, dark and threatening: I was destined once more to be dashed on hidden shoals, and swallowed up in an unfathomable abyss.

A series of wet weather, towards the latter end of the summer, destroyed the hopes of our harvest: unusual exertions, added to mental anxiety and exposure to the inclement elements, affected the health of James, on whom age was now rapidly advancing, and brought on a tertian ague: he became every day more debilitated, and, at length, utterly unable to quit his chamber. My attendance upon my friend, fatigue, and watching, unfitted me for performing the duties of my station; every thing wore a menacing aspect, and ruin approached with hasty strides. I endeavoured to conceal from my patient, lest I should aggravate his sufferings, the increasing untoward state of our affairs, and still wore in his presence a cheerful aspect. To supply a present exigence, I prevailed, with some difficulty, on a wealthy neighbour to grant me the loan of fifteen pounds, for which, at his request, I gave him a written acknowledgement.

A few days subsequent to this transaction, after passing the night by the bedside of my friend, the morning beaming with unusual brilliancy, I walked into the fields to give some directions to the labourers and to observe their progress. The serenity of the weather, the stillness of the hour, and the freshness of the early breeze, inducing me to prolong my ramble, I was joined in my way by a party of the village-children, who had been nutting, and who hastened to present to me a share of their spoil. We had proceeded through a copse, the little peasants carelessly laughing and chatting, when, in the midst of their gambols, we were startled by the report of a fowling-piece at no great distance, and, in a short time after, through a break in the hedge which bordered our path, some dogs appeared. One of the younger children, in attempting a leap which exceeded its powers, had fallen, and slightly wounded itself: attempting to sooth it, I had seated myself on a bank, and, tenderly leaning over the child, observed not the sportsmen, who were by this time advancing towards the little group. A confused murmur among the children, that seemed to indicate respect, announced their approach, and roused my attention. Suddenly raising my eyes, and starting from the bank, I beheld, leaning on his gun, and intently gazing upon me, the lord of the manor, my old adversary, Sir Peter Osborne!

I shrieked involuntarily, staggered backward, and was sinking to the ground, when, catching me in his arms, he prevented my fall. A convulsive trembling shook my limbs; while, petrified with horror, and unable to speak, I continued to gaze wildly on this terrible apparition, my strength utterly failing me, and my senses wholly bewildered. A gentleman by whom he was accompanied, observing my disordered appearance, procured water from a neighbouring brook, plentifully sprinkling my neck and face. The children crowded around me, helpless and terrified: some labourers, alarmed by their cries, hastened to my relief, to whom the hated Osborne having consigned me, precipitately vanished from my sight.

Near an hour elapsed ere I had the power to remove from this fatal spot, where I had been transfixed, as it were, by the glance of the basilisk. My whole frame appeared to have suffered a revulsion: pale, trembling, languid, leaning upon two of the elder children, I regained with difficulty my home. Unwilling to wound the gentle nature of my friend by a relation of the past scene, I retired to my chamber, wept in secret, and sought to calm my disordered spirits.

For three succeeding days, I was assailed by letters

and messages from our landlord: the former were returned unopened; to the latter no reply was vouchsafed.
On the fourth evening a man muffled in a horseman's
coat requested to speak with me on urgent business that
imported my life and honour. A young girl, whom I had
hired to assist me in my household cares during the illness
of my good James, brought me this account. Suspecting
but too truly the guileful betrayer, I resolutely refused to
appear. A new and more importunate message reiterated
the request, which provoked from me a refusal still more
peremptory and decisive.

Several weeks elapsed, and, hearing no farther from
my persecutor, I began again to breathe freely. The oppression of terror from the late rencontre was gradually
removed from my heart; the health of my friend appeared
to mend, though slowly; seed-time approached with a
more favourable aspect; the heavens cleared; and the
drooping spirits of the husbandmen began to revive.

"Courage, my lass!" cried James exulting. "Another
year, if the 'squire has patience with us, may retrieve the
losses of this, and bring all matters right again."

I resumed the business of my dairy with diligence; the
elastic vigour of my mind revived, and my bosom dilated
with hope; but, alas! my intervals of repose were destined
to be but as the light breeze of summer, which refreshes
tha air but for a moment! Suddenly I found myself
shunned by my acquaintance, as one infected by a pesti-
lence: every eye scowled on me, every neck was scornfully
averted on my approach. The young peasants, who had
been accustomed to pay me homage, leered and tittered
as I passed; and the village-maidens, bridling, shunned
every familiar courtesy or advance. The source of this
change was soon apparent, when I beheld, mingled with
the rustics in their sports, the pampered lackeys of my

powerful foe. These insults became at length too pointed and insupportable to be longer concealed from my friend, whose weak state little fitted him for the disclosure: added to which, I was now daily importuned by our neighbour for the debt which I had incurred; while he scrupled not, with gross hints and coarse language, to suggest, that an equivalent might be accepted for a loan I professed myself unable to repay. The scorn and indignation which I was incapable of repressing drew upon me bitter sarcasms, and menaces that he would no longer be the dupe of my fair face and whining hypocrisy.

Harassed and perplexed on every side, what was now to be done? — Should I repair to the residence of the principal inhabitants of the village, and narrate succinctly to them the wrongs and the calamities of my past life? A perilous expedient! for, what credit has the simple asseverations of the sufferer, sole witness in his own cause, to look for against the poison of detraction, the influence of wealth and power, the bigotry of prejudice, the virulence of envy, the spleen and the corruption engendered in the human mind by barbarous institutions and pernicious habits?

The kind-hearted James listened, while I imparted to him these melancholy particulars, with an emotion that redoubled my distress: it seemed as if exhausted nature was unequal to the sustaining of any accumulation to a burthen that had before pressed on him but too heavily. A sudden change appeared in his countenance, his features became distorted, he uttered a hollow groan, and his limbs sunk lifeless; while, catching him in my arms, I prevented his falling from his chair. His eyes were fixed on mine, as, shuddering, I essayed to support him, with a tender and mournful expression: he tried in vain to speak, while palsy seized his faultering frame. Abandoning myself to agonized grief, I rent the air with piercing cries: the neighbours, alarmed by my shrieks, hastened to our assistance, but vain were all their cares, vain my assiduities, my sorrow, my despair; on the third succeeding morning, my friend, my second father, breathed, in my arms, his last sigh.

The sluices of my heart were now opened; I poured forth torrents of grateful, filial tears; till, exhausted by the vehemence of my emotions, I sunk into listless, stubborn sadness.

The effects of my deceased friend, consisting merely of simple furniture and implements of husbandry, were, after his internment, taken possession of by the steward of our landlord, to whom they of right appertained, for arrears of rent and payment of the bond given in default of the original contract. I passively beheld these transactions, in which I seemed to take no interest: a heavy stupor weighed down my spirits, till I was roused from this oppression by the appearance of Sir Peter Osborne, who, after affecting to condole with me on my loss, endeavouring to insinuate himself into my confidence, and making vague offers of service, presuming on my deplorable situation, his passion inflamed by opposition, artfully contrived to introduce his former pretensions, now become, if possible, more than ever odious to me. Finding me deaf to his solicitations, and frenzied by his insults, his heart appeared to relent, and his purposes seemed suspended. Humbling himself before me, he implored my forgiveness, cursed the consequences of his barbarous acts (consequences, he swore, alike unforeseen and deprecated,) and besought me, with apparent sincerity, to accept the only recompense in his power to bestow, — a *legal* title to his hand and fortune.

"Restore to me, if you can," exclaimed I, with a vehemence almost frantic, irritated by my sufferings, "my fame, my honour, *my friend*, my unbroken mind, and un- sullied youth; then might you, indeed, talk of your con- trition; then might you dare to propose amends for my sorrows. O wretch!" continued I with increasing fervour, "unprincipled and selfish voluptuary! what havoc has your criminal passion wrought! Think not that I would ally my soul to your's; my haughty spirit, wounded, but not crushed, utterly contemns you; in every light, contemns you. Blast not my sight by your presence; mock not the woes you have heaped upon my defenceless head. Pitiless man, death will, ere long, free me from your persecutions! Wearied with calamity, my strength spent in fruitless strug- gles, I have no reverse to hope for, no favours to ask, and, from you, will receive none. I yield to my destiny; I am content to die. Whether through the palace or the dungeon lies the passage to the chambers of death it im- ports not. Go! leave me to my fate! Indulge not yourself in beholding the ruin you have made. Suffer me (it is all I ask!) but to die decently and alone."

As I ceased to speak, I covered my face with my hand- kerchief, reclining my head on my hands in mournful and determined silence. Perceiving expostulation and entreaty alike fruitless, he at length rose, imploring me to allow reflection to mitigate the passionate sense of my wrongs, and induce me to accept their honourable recompense. In the mean time, he pressed me to permit him to become my banker. Early in the ensuing morning, he assured me, it was his intention to set out for London, (since he found, at present, he must not hope to soften me in his favour,) whence he should immediately depart to fulfil an engage- ment with a friend, whom he had promised to accompany in a tour to the western islands.[51] He should probably be absent some months: on his return, he trusted to find that time had produced on the asperity of my present feelings its healing effects. He again, on retiring, urged me to accept a bank-bill, which I obstinately persisted to refuse.

The next day, with a kind of sullen desperation, I prepared for my departure from the farm, where I had flattered myself with spending in peace the remainder of a disastrous life. I had no determined plan; I seemed about to commit myself, without purpose or reflection, to my remorseless destiny. The young woman who had occasionally assisted me in my household cares still remained with me, affectionately mingling her tears with mine. As she was busied in making the little preparations for my journey, she suddenly uttered an exclamation of joy, and, running towards me, put into my hand a fifty-pound bank-note, which Sir Peter had, as I conjectured, on the preceding evening, slipped into a small port-folio, in which I had been accustomed to preserve my drawings. I immediately formed my resolution; but, unwilling to damp the rapture of the artless girl on this discovery, though my surprise was manifest, I concealed from her my suspicion and my design, (fatal tenderness!) and, after depositing the note carefully in my pocket-book, and making, from my scanty wardrobe, some little presents to my kind friend, set forward on my forlorn expedition.

I proceeded slowly to the next market-town, about seven miles distance from the village, in a state of anxiety and irresolution; where, procuring a homely lodging, I determined to remain for the night. Having enclosed the note in a blank paper, and addressed it to Sir Peter's house in town, I delivered it to the mail, a sentiment of mingled heroism and despair still sustaining me. In the morning I pursued my way, unknowing and almost regardless whither I went, intent only on escaping the cry of infamy, that,

"Gathering in the wind,
"Still shew'd my instant foes behind."[52]

I had scarcely got out of the town when the sound of a
horse's feet induced me to turn. The rider called loudly to
me to stop, and, hastening towards me, informed me that
he had a *writ* against me, which I must immediately discharge, or return with him, and take up my lodging in the
county-gaol. Gasping with terror, it was some minutes before I could fully comprehend the nature of this arrest. In
the late confusion and distress of my thoughts, I had wholly
forgotten the debt which I had contracted during the illness
of my friend. My creditor, on the rumour of my having departed from the village, enriched, as reported by my simple
indiscreet friend, by the bounty of some unknown benefactor, whose name he was at no loss to conjecture, conceived
this a proper time to procure the repayment of the sum due
to him. My steps were easily traced; and, on professing my
utter inability to discharge the debt, I was hurried back, and
thrown into the county-gaol, overwhelmed with obloquy
and disgrace. In vain I endeavoured to justify myself; my
character blasted, no one believed the tale I told; every ear
was shut, every heart was hardened, against me. It was suspected that I had either unaccountably disposed of, or had
secreted, the note, relying for my deliverance on my tears
and my eloquence. — My incensed creditor resolved to re-
venge himself for my former disdain, and, at least, to detain
me in confinement till the return of the 'squire, who, from
the past transactions, he doubted not would cheerfully liberate me.

Four months of uninterrupted solitude have since
elapsed; the winter has far advanced; the damp and un-

wholesome air of my apartment has communicated rheu-
matic pains to my limbs; the vigour of my frame begins
to yield to the depredations of grief, the inactivity of my
situation, and the mephitic[53] vapour that surrounds me.
Indulged with pen and paper, I have sought to beguile
my woes by tracing their origin and their progress. I an-
ticipate, with magnanimity, their termination: my spirit,
which I have searched and probed, acquits me of intentional error. Involved, as by a fatal mechanism, in the
infamy of my wretched mother, thrown into similar circumstances, and looking to a catastrophe little less fearful,
I have still the consolation of remembering that I suffered
not despair to plunge my soul in crime, that I braved the
shocks of fortune, eluded the snares of vice, and struggled
in the trammels of prejudice with dauntless intrepidity.
But *it avails me not!* I sink beneath a torrent, whose resistless waves overwhelm alike in a common ruin the guiltless
and the guilty.

A deadly torpor steals over my faculties; principles
loosen in my clouded mind; my heart, formed for tender
sympathies, for social affections, withers in joyless, hopeless solitude; my beauty fades as the yellow leaf in autumn;
my confidence in humanity totters to its base; virtue appears to me an empty name; the current of life creeps
slowly, wasted by inanity and clogged by disease. Why
should I drain the embittered cup, – why exhaust life's
wretched dregs, – why shiver, like a dastard, on the brink
of dissolution, – when enjoyment, activity, usefulness,
hope, *are lost for ever?* – Despair nerves my hand; despair
justifies the deed. O God of truth! (if priests belie thee
not;) O God of truth and love! – I can no more; my
quivering fingers drop the pen! – Posterity, receive my
last appeal!

Conclusion

TWO TEDIOUS YEARS have worn away, since, urged by despair, I desperately determined to cut short with life its calamities; yet I drag on a joyless existence, and, while life ebbs daily, approach, by lingering steps, the tomb. Welcome, thrice welcome, quiet asylum! whither my wishes hourly tend; where passion no longer racks the heart; where darkness shrouds, where slander and persecution pause and leave their victim; where disappointment and sorrow never enter!

In the hour of agony, when, wearied by accumulated griefs, reason faultered and nature yielded, my purpose was on a sudden suspended by the murmur of voices and the sound of footsteps, that appeared to approach the chamber in which I was confined, the door of which, in a few moments, precipitately flew open. Confused and bewildered, I seemed to have no distinct perception, till a piercing shriek recalled my faculties, when I found myself folded in the arms of Mrs. Neville, the tender friend of my youth. Her husband, by whom she was accompanied, at the same time advancing towards me, took my hand, while, pressing it cordially, he addressed me in accents of commiseration, and sought to rouse my benumbed powers. I neither spoke nor wept, but continued to gaze in silence, alternately, on the features of my friends, on the gaoler, who conducted them, and on the instrument of destruction, which had fallen from my nerveless hand.

"Dearest Mary," repeated Mr. Neville, in a tone of mingled pity and horror, while the tear glistened on his manly cheek, "you are free! your sufferings are at an end!"

I smiled incredulously, and shook my head. He went on: — "Speak to the friends who love you! in the hour of

169

whose distress you interposed like a ministering angel! who come to liberate you, to repay into your bosom a hundred-fold your generous kindness! Suffer not an ingenuous shame to overwhelm you. Who is free from error? Habitual depravity can never sink a soul like your's. Come, and share with us our prosperity; we will shelter you from a cruel, undistinguishing world: we will smooth, will assist, your return to virtue."

Mrs. Neville, as her husband ceased speaking, embraced me again and again; pressed to her bosom my icy hands, my languid frame; and, by the mute eloquence of tender endearment, at length melted my stubborn spirit. I dissolved into a flood of tears, that seemed to quench my burning brain, and suffered myself to be led, or rather borne, by my friends, to a chaise that waited to convey us from the prison, my emotions still swelling too high for utterance.

Many weeks I was confined to a chamber of sickness, and it was by slow degrees that I was enabled to disclose the tale of my woes. I experienced from my benevolent hosts every kind attention, every tender sympathy; but the tone of my mind was destroyed, and the springs of life were sapped. It seemed as if a premature old age had withered my bloom and blasted the vigour of my youth: no longer robust, sanguine, active, broken spirits and a shattered constitution sunk me to the weakness of infancy, imaginary terrors haunted my mind, and a complication of nameless depressing pangs racked my frame.

My friends informed me, that, on their arrival in England, they had learned, from a person whom my deceased guardian had been accustomed to employ as an agent in his pecuniary concerns, to whom they were indebted for the five hundred pounds which had enabled them to accept an appointment, from which they had acquired a competence sufficiently liberal to induce them to return to their native land. Some little time previous to his death, Mr. Raymond had communicated to this man the particulars of his benefaction to his friends in the crisis of their distress, charging him never to reveal this circumstance, unless the prosperity and return of Mr. Neville, or any disaster that might befal me, should render the concealment altogether unjustifiable: the rumour of my disgrace and misfortunes had reached this person, who, accidentally hearing, within a short period, of the arrival of Mr. Neville with his family, conceived this a proper time to fulfil the commission entrusted to him, and accordingly waited on my friends for that purpose. Instantly hastening to my relief, they omitted nothing that might serve to convince me of their grateful affection.

Mr. Neville also hinted, that he had some reason to suspect he had been indebted to the interest of Sir Peter Osborne for his appointment abroad. That gentleman, he conjectured, being aware of the declining health of my guardian, had taken this step with a view of forwarding his designs upon my innocence, by depriving me of protection or resource.

For twelve months, I fluctuated between life and death; disappointment, confinement, unwholesome air, mental anguish, had combined to exhaust and ravage my frame: a burthen to myself, and an affliction to my friends, the body survived, but the spirit was fled: I seemed to endure a living death, when affection and humanity once more roused me to a temporary, a last exertion.

In a chill, humid autumn, Mr. Neville contracted, from repeated colds which he had neglected, a threatening disorder, which, in a few weeks, terminated fatally. During his illness, his wife never quitted him for a moment: a preternatural strength and courage appeared to sustain her, till, at the instant when he breathed in her arms his last sigh, she sunk upon his lifeless remains in a swoon, which, on her revival, was succeeded by a stupor, that, after some days, gave place to insanity. Her piercing shrieks, her pathetic appeals, her heart-rending exclamations, her wild anguish, the despair painted in her eyes, her frantic exertions, are ever present to my remembrance. Regardless of my own increasing weakness, I watched her incessantly, presented to her her children, and sought in vain to calm the agonies of her spirit. Her feeble frame yielded to the unequal conflict; she survived her husband but a short period. Some hours previous to her dissolution, an interval of sanity occurred, in which, calling me to her pillow and grasping my hand, she gave brief directions for the consignment of her children, whom she enfolded in a last maternal embrace, to the care of a relation, appointed, by Mr. Neville, as the executor of his worldly affairs.

"You, my beloved Mary," continued she, "will not long survive your friends: over your stronger mind, *injustice* has triumphed, and consigned you to an early grave; while I sink a feeble victim to an *excessive*, and therefore blameable, tenderness. My husband was worthy of my affection; but I adored him with a fondness too lavish, an idolatrous devotion, in which every other duty has been at length absorbed. This enthusiasm clouded even my brightest moments with sadness: my confidence in my beloved Neville, who never for a moment wounded my heart by intentional unkindness, knew no bounds; yet it was not possible that his firmer mind should be able to conceive the excess of my sensibility; the keen pangs, the torturing solicitude, which a momentary absence, the slightest circumstance, the most casual word, or inadvertent gesture, would, at times, inflict on my soul. Every accident, even the vicissitudes of the seasons, alarmed me, lest they should impair the health of him on whose welfare my very being seemed suspended. If a transient paleness faded his cheek, my bosom throbbed with apprehension; if thought or care clouded his brow, a thousand inquietudes racked my heart. Even the blessing of his affection I held with a perpetual and fearful distrust, lest, by demerit or by any unguarded conduct, I should unwittingly forfeit it. Yet these weaknesses, alike fostered and lamented, which I had not the strength to subdue, I carefully sought to hide in the bottom of my heart; and, while that heart repined in secret, subjected my conduct to the severest discipline. LOVE, that created these exquisite refinements, assisted me to stifle them, lest they should wound the peace of him for whom alone I breathed, — to promote whose happiness seemed to be the only *end* of my existence. I sought in his eyes to read and to prevent his wishes; I modelled to his my temper, my character, my words, my actions, even the expression of my feelings. I had no individual existence; my very being was absorbed in that of my husband. All the worth, all the talent, all the powers of my mind, were the product of my affection, that, founded upon a conviction of worth, was nurtured in solitude and cemented by time and habit. I was the slave, and am at length become the victim, of my tenderness. LOVE was the vital spark that animated my frame, that sustained my being; it is extinguished, and *I follow to the tomb its object.* Farewel, my friend! Amidst thy own unmerited sufferings pause a moment, and embalm with one tender tear the grave of thy friend! Let my dust mingle with that of my beloved husband; and may our spirits unite in purer regions!"

As my friend pronounced these last words, a transient fire beamed in her eyes, while a faint flush overspread her wan cheek. It instantly faded, and — *she spoke no more!*

Tender and gentle spirit! unfitted for this rude world, deprived of its support, thy fragile form yielded to the first rough blast of disappointment! I have performed thy dying request; I have delivered thy children to the protection of their relation; I have interred thy remains in the same grave with those of thy husband; I have watered with my tears the turf which covers them!

Accelerated by these painful duties, the disorder which has gradually wasted my strength and sapped the powers of life gains hourly ground. My days curtailed in their prime, I perceive, without terror or regret, while the current of my blood freezes, the approach of dissolution.

Almighty Nature, mysterious are thy decrees! — The vigorous promise of my youth has failed. The victim of a barbarous prejudice, society has cast me out from its bosom. The sensibilities of my heart have been turned to bitterness, the powers of my mind wasted, my projects rendered abortive, my virtues and my sufferings alike unrewarded, *I have lived in vain!* unless the story of my sorrows should kindle in the heart of man, in behalf of my oppressed sex, the sacred claims of humanity and justice. From the fate of my wretched mother (in which, alas! my own has been involved,) let him learn, that, while the slave of sensuality, inconsistent as assuming, he pours, by *his conduct*, contempt upon chastity, in vain will he impose on *woman* barbarous penalties, or seek to multiply restrictions; his seductions and example, yet more powerful, will defeat his precepts, of which *hypocrisy*, not virtue, is the genuine fruit. Ignorance and despotism, combating frailty with cruelty, may go on to propose *partial* reform in one invariable, melancholy, round; reason derides the weak effort; while the fabric of superstition and crime, extending its broad base, mocks the toil of the visionary projector.

NOTES

Explanatory Notes

Volume I

1. (Titlepage) Epigraph: *Moore's Female Seducers* Edward Moore (1712–1757) published *Fables for the Female Sex* (1744) with the assistance of Henry Brooke (1703–1783). This collection of sixteen fables was extremely popular and frequently reprinted throughout the eighteenth and into the nineteenth century. Fable XV, "The Female Seducers" begins: "'Tis said of widow, maid and wife,/That honour is a woman's life." It warns women that "the wounds of honour never close." The passage beginning "Her trumpet slander rais'd on high" occurs near the end after the chaste maiden of the fable loses her innocence. As she no longer owns that "form divine," she turns to heaven who welcomes the "lovely penitent." (Edward Moore, *Fables for the Female Sex*, 3rd ed. London: T. Davies & J. Dodsley, 1766, pp. 115–148).

2. (p. 1) *a former publication* In the preface to *Memoirs of Emma Courtney* (1796) Hays tells her readers: "bear in mind, that the errors of my heroine were the offspring of sensibility; and that the result of her hazardous experiment is calculated to operate as a *warning*, rather than as an example" (Pandora xviii).

3. (p. 1) *the cry of slander was raised against me* After the pub-

177

lication of *Emma Courtney*, Hays was attacked by various anti-Jacobins such as Charles Lloyd, Elizabeth Hamilton, and the Reverend Richard Polwhele.

4.   (p. 1) *too-great stress laid on the reputation for chastity* Similar comments are made by Mary Wollstonecraft. See *A Vindication of the Rights of Woman*, ch. VIII "Morality Undermined by Sexual Notions of the Importance of a Good Reputation." Catherine Macaulay in *Letters on Education* (1790) stresses the importance of chastity: "But the most difficult part of female education, is to give girls such an idea of chastity, as shall arm their reason and their sentiments on the side of useful virtue" (Letter XXIV).

5.   (p. 3) *the gloomy walls of a prison* Mary Wollstonecraft's *The Wrongs of Woman, or Maria* (1798) also opens with the heroine immured in a "dreary cell" (Oxford World's Classics 76).

6.   (p. 3) *a Being existeth, who searcheth the heart, and judgeth not as man judgeth* Jeremiah 17:10 I the Lord search the heart, I try the reins, even to give every man according to his ways, and according to the fruit of his doings.

I Samuel 16:7 The Lord does not see as man sees; men judge by appearances but the Lord judges by the heart.

7.   (p. 3) *victim of despotism, oppression, or error, tenant of a dungeon* Hays is deliberately using politically sensitive language here as many novelists of the 1790s did. As Ronald Paulson notes: "by the time *The Mysteries of Udolpho* (1794) appeared, the castle, prison, tyrant, and sensitive young girl could no longer be presented naïvely; they had all been familiarized and sophisticated by the events in France," *Representations of Revolution (1789–1820)* (221).

8.   (p. 5) *sensibility* used here, would be the power or faculty of feeling, capacity of sensation and emotion as distinguished from cognition and will.

9.   (p. 5) *Monmouthshire* in South Wales. The town Monmouth is located at the confluence of the Rivers Wye and Monnow. The region, roughly bordering the Usk Valley in the west, the Wye Valley in the east, and Bristol Channel to the south, is pleasingly diversified. A portion is mountainous and rocky, but the rich land in the valleys and hills is full of woods and pastures.

10.   (p. 5) *a robust constitution, a cultivated understanding, and a vigorous intellect* Hays disagrees with Rousseau who in *Émile* argued that girls were more delicate, and should be educated differently than boys. She agrees with Wollstonecraft that the bodies of girls should be strengthened by outdoor exercise. See *A Vindication of the Rights of Woman*, Chapter II "The Prevailing Opinion of a Sexual Character Discussed."

11.   (p. 6) *a material link in the chain of events* The desire to analyze the past and childhood of the heroine is due to William Godwin's influence and views on "necessitarianism." Godwin argues that "the characters of men originate in their external circumstances," *Enquiry Concerning Political Justice*, ed. K. Codell Carter (Clarendon 1793 I:iv, 27). In a piece on "The Talents of Women," in *The Monthly Magazine* (July 1796):469–470, "a woman," probably Hays, cites Godwin's *Political Justice*: "that the actions and dispositions of men are not the offspring of any original bias that they bring into the world, . . . but flow entirely from the operation of circumstances and events acting upon a faculty of receiving sensible

impressions, that all our knowledge, all our ideas, everything we possess as intelligent beings, comes from impression."

12.　(p. 6) *the rudiments of the French, Italian, and Latin, languages; in the elements of geometry, algebra, and arithmetic* Like Mary Wollstonecraft, Catherine Macaulay, and Hannah More, Hays wanted women to learn more than just ornamental skills usually consisting of dress, drawing, music and a few phrases of French or Italian. Here Hays shows the heroine cultivating her mind as well as her body. Wollstonecraft's *Thoughts on the Education of Daughters* (1788) lamented the fact that females, fashionably educated, had few "modes of earning a subsistence," while Hannah More's *Strictures on the Modern System of Female Education* (1799) argued that "the chief end to be proposed in cultivating the understandings of women, is to qualify them for the practical purposes of life" (Chapter XIII).

13.　(p. 7) *a post-coach* a stage-coach used for carrying mail, a mail-coach, a stage coach generally, or a coach that runs on specified days between two places for the conveyance of passengers, parcels, etc. (*OED*).

14.　(p. 11) *curious* archaic or obsolete for bestowing care or pains; careful, studious, attentive.

15.　(p. 14) *caught you in the fact* in the very act; in the 16th and 17th century, usually an evil deed, a crime.

16.　(p. 14) *a Hebe* Hebe is the daughter of Zeus and Hera according to Hesiod, and appears in Homer's *Iliad* (Book 4) as the cup-bearer of the gods.

17.   (p. 23) *in the cause of right, we should contemn bodily pain* In
       Enquiry Concerning Political Justice (1793) William Godwin
       argues that pain is the last resort: "though there is some
       pain, or absolute evil, which, relatively taken, must be ad-
       mitted to be attended with an overbalance of good, yet it
       is a matter of great delicacy and difficulty, in most in-
       stances, to decide in favour of pain, which, whatever be its
       relative value, is certainly a negative quantity to be de-
       ducted in the sum total of happiness. (Clarendon IV:xi,
       191).

18.   (p. 25) *enthusiastic love of science and literature* In Hays'
       Emma Courtney, Emma also studies subjects not usually
       taught to females: "science . . . astronomy and philosophy
       . . . languages, . . . criticism and grammar, and the rules of
       composition" (Pandora 71).   Hays believed that women
       could and should learn more than needlework and lan-
       guages.   Emma resents her boarding school where she says,
       "I was obliged to sit poring over needle work, and forbidden
       to prate; — my body was tortured into forms, my mind co-
       erced, and talks imposed upon me, grammar and French,
       mere words, that conveyed to one no ideas" (Pandora 14).

       In *Letters and Essays, Moral and Miscellaneous* (1793) Hays says:
       "of all bondage, mental bondage [is] the most fatal . . . the un-
       derstanding of women have been chained down to frivolity
       and trifles, and have increased the general tide of effemi-
       nacy and corruption" (19).   Similarly in *Appeal to the Men of
       Great Britain* she laments: "Thus, many a good head is stuffed
       with ribbons, gauze, fringes, flounces, and furbelows that
       might have received and communicated far other and more
       noble impressions.   And many a fine imagination has been ex-
       hausted upon these, which had they been turned to the study
       of nature, or initiated into the dignified embellishments of the

fine arts, might have adorned, delighted, and improved society" (79). Many "arts" have been employed to keep
women "in a state of PERPETUAL BABYISM" (97).

19.　　(p. 28) *Of extraordinary talents, like diamonds of uncommon*
magnitude, it has been truly said, calculation cannot find the
value Thomas Holcroft's *Anna St. Ives* (1792) is a Jacobin
novel that attempted to transgress class barriers by having
the heroine, a baronet's daughter, love and marry the son
of her father's steward who is a brave and intelligent man
and a sincere reformer. A variation of the passage is found
at the end of the novel: "What is there precious but mind?
And when mind, like a diamond of uncommon growth, ex-
ceeds a certain magnitude, calculation cannot find its
value!" (*Anna St. Ives*, ed. Peter Faulkner, London: Oxford
UP, 1970, p. 481).

20.　　(p. 28) *vivid sensations, exquisite sensibilities, powerful energies,*
and imperious passions Hays' *Emma Courtney* has a similar
passage on the misdirected energies of intelligent women:
"While men pursue interest, honor, pleasure, as accords
with several dispositions, women, who have too much delicacy, sense, and spirit, to degrade themselves by the vilest
of all interchanges, remain insulated beings, and must be
content tamely to look on, without taking part in the great,
though often absurd and tragical drama of life. Hence the
eccentricities of conduct, with which women of superior
minds have been accused — the struggles, the despairing
though generous struggles of an ardent spirit, denied a
scope for its exertions" (Pandora 86).

Similarly in *Appeal to the Men of Great Britain in Behalf of*
Women Hays writes: "Alas! What can women be expected
to do? Driven and excluded from what are commonly es-

teemed the consequential offices of life; — denied, and perhaps with reason and propriety too, any political existence;
— and literary talents and acquirements, nay genius itself,
being in them generally regarded rather with contempt or
jealousy, than meeting with encouragement and applause;
— nothing in short being left for them, but domestic duties,
and superficial accomplishments and vanities — Is it surpris-
ing, that instead of doing as men bid them . . . that spoiled
by prosperity and goaded on by temptation and the allurements of pleasure, they give a loose rein to their passions,
and plunge headlong into folly and dissipation; regardless
in an eminent degree of their family, their fame, and their
fortune?" (81–2)

In *Rights of Woman* Wollstonecraft says: "Women have sel-
dom sufficient serious employment to silence their feelings;
a round of little cares, or vain pursuits frittering away all
strength of mind and organs, they become naturally only
objects of sense. — In short, the whole tenour of female
education. . . tends to render the best disposed romantic
and inconstant; and the remainder vain and mean" (Norton
75).

21.   (p. 29) *rendered you useful to society . . . triumph over the imperious demands of passion* In "Reform or Ruin," Mitzi Myers
points out that Wollstonecraft and Hannah More "both
strive to replace the regnant ideal of pliant, unproductive
urbanity with socially functional middle-class models," *Studies in Eighteenth-Century Culture* 11 (1982):199–216. Hays
shows Mr. Raymond here attempting to give Mary an education that would make her "useful" to society.

22.   (p. 32) *man of the world* In 1773 Henry Mackenzie published *The Man of the World,* a novel whose rakish hero Sir
Thomas Sindall is the opposite of the idealized Harley in

The Man of Feeling (1771). Sindall, a libertine in the tradition of Richardson's Lovelace in *Clarissa,* drugs and rapes Harriet, a young woman in his neighborhood. Many years later he attempts to seduce his ward, Lucy, not knowing that she is his daughter through his liaison with Harriet.

23.   (p. 35) *When reason, virtue, nature sanctify its emotions* The heroine of *Emma Courtney* similarly questions conventions and customs of society which prevent her lover from acknowledging his affections for her. She claims her attachment to Augustus, "sanctioned by nature, reason, and virtue," ennobles the "mind capable of conceiving and cherishing it" (Pandora 80).

24.   (p. 38) *on a curacy of sixty pounds a year* This amount is very modest. J.H. Plumb, *England in the Eighteenth Century* (Harmondsworth: Penguin, 1950), estimates that in the early part of the century, a village curacy of around £40 was on the lowest rung of the ladder of preferment. The *London Advertiser* of 1786 calculated the average household expenses for a family with four children and two maids to be around £400, but stated that a family could survive at £200 a year. See Walter Besant, *London in the Eighteenth Century* (London: Adam & Charles Black, 1902, pp. 303–304).

25.   (p. 38) *canker most pernicious to every virtue is dependence; and the most fatal species of bondage is subjection to the demands of our own imperious passions* Dependence and the demands of passions are concerns present in Hays' first novel. Emma Courtney abhorred the condition of dependence: "The small pittance bequeathed to me was insufficient to preserve me from dependence . . . . I felt my heart die within me" (Pandora 31). The heroine, as Hays describes her in the Preface, is "a human being, loving virtue while

enslaved by passion" (xviii).

Mary Wollstonecraft, in *A Vindication of the Rights of Woman,* makes a comparable statement about female dependence: "Men have superior strength of body, but were it not for mistaken notions of beauty, women would acquire sufficient to enable them to earn their own subsistence, the true definition of independence, and to bear those bodily inconveniences and exertions that are requisite to strengthen the mind" (Norton 85).

26. (p. 41) *a chaise* a light open carriage for one or two persons, for pleasure or travelling, often having a top or calash; those with four wheels resembling the phaeton, those with two the curricle.

27. (p. 41) *halcyon* calm, peaceful, happy, prosperous.

28. (p. 42) *casement* hinged window or part of window.

29. (p. 43) *hair unsoiled by powder* wearing wigs and powdering one's hair were common practices in the early and mid-eighteenth century. By the late eighteenth century, leaving off hair powder was coming into fashion as part of a reformist trend to "naturalness." Among the minor "Miseries of Life" of the period is the slipping and sliding of lumps of powder and pomatum from the head down to the plate at dinner. Hair was cut short to evade the duty of powder.

30. (p. 46) *annual income of sixty pounds* see note 24.

31. (p. 46) *product of a well-planted garden, and the profits of a few acres of land, cultivated by the labour of the worthy curate* This ideal of the self-sufficient cottage retreat was becoming popular and appears in eighteenth-century works in various

forms. See the ending of Voltaire's *Candide* (1759) where the hero and his friends decide to content themselves with the cultivation of their little garden, and the ending of Elizabeth Inchbald's *Nature and Art* (1796) where the hero and his wife also retreat to a pastoral, idyllic cottage to avoid the contamination of the corrupt society.

32.   (p. 50) *in a gay livery* wearing a particular suit of clothes or badge bestowed by a person upon his retainers or servants to serve as a token by which they may be recognized.

33.   (p. 55) *nature, reason and virtue* the qualities Hays most often uses in opposition to the customs and trammels of society. See note 23.

34.   (p. 56) *We loved each other; we beheld only our mutual perfections . . . . we imposed upon ourselves an honourable sacrifice that added a zest to our happiness* Jean-Jacques Rousseau's *Émile* was first published in 1762 and translated several times into English. The passage Hays quotes is a description of the sublime love between Emilius and Sophia: "There is no doubt but they converse on that subject, pleased with its illusion; they see their own perfections, they love one another, and they are led by a kind of enthusiasm to discourse on the reward of virtue. The sacrifices they offer up at his altar render it dear to them. In the midst of some of their transports, which they are obliged to restrain, they mingle their tears; tears purer than the dew of heaven, tears so delicious, as to create the most exquisite rapture; in short, they are in the most bewitching delirium that the human mind is capable of enjoying. Even their denials are an honourable sacrifice, and make an addition to their happiness." *Émilius; or, A Treatise of Education* (Edinburgh: J. Dickson & C. Elliot, 1773), volume 3, bk. V, 164–165.

35.   (p. 63) *sophistical pretences* from sophism, false arguments, especially one intended to deceive.

36.   (p. 66) *Took off the rose/ From the fair forehead of an innocent love,/ And plac'd a blister there.* William Shakespeare, *Hamlet* (F1-1623): "...takes off the Rose/ From the faire forehead of an innocent love,/ And makes a blister there" (III, iv, 42–44).

37.   (p. 67) *remorse, with its serpent-sting* John Dryden's translation of *Lucretius*: "Then sharp remorse shoots out her angry sting" (IV:113).

John Milton, *Samson Agonistes* (1671): "And secret sting of amorous remorse" (l. 1007).

38.   (p. 68) *I committed it to paper* Putting down her life story in jail, Mary's mother would be writing a type of confessional narrative, or criminal autobiography following the tradition of Puritan spiritual autobiographies, except that moral conscience has taken the place of the spiritual here. A well-known example of this genre would be Daniel Defoe's *Roxana* (1724). See G.A. Starr, *Defoe and Spiritual Autobiography* (Princeton UP, 1965).

Volume II

39.   (p. 99) *I can exert my talents for my support, or procure a sustenance by the labour of my hands* Hays has written on the difficulty of single women finding employment and becoming independent in *Emma Courtney*: "Cruel prejudices! I exclaimed — hapless woman! Why was I not educated for commerce, for a profession, for labour? Why have I been

rendered feeble and delicate by bodily constraint, and fastidious by artificial refinement? Why are we bound, by the
habits of society, as with an adamantine chain? Why do we
suffer ourselves to be confined within a magic circle, without daring, by a magnanimous effort, to dissolve the barbarous spell?" (Pandora 31).

Similarly, Mary Wollstonecraft's Jemima in *The Wrongs of
Woman* (1797) says: "How often have I heard . . . in conversation, and read in books that every person willing to
work may find employment? It is the vague assertion, I believe, of insensible indolence, when it relates to men; but
with respect to women, I am sure of its fallacy, unless they
will submit to the most menial bodily labour; and even to
be employed at hard labour is out of the reach of many,
whose reputation misfortune or folly has tainted (Oxford
World's Classics 114).

40.   (p. 104) *Drown'd, all drown'd,/ In that great sea which nothing
disembogues* source unknown.

41.   (p. 109) *stage-coach* a coach that keeps its stages; a coach that
passes and repasses on certain days for the accommodation of
passengers (Samuel Johnson, *Dictionary of the English Language*).

42.   (p. 110) St. James's Street a street in the west end of London
which begins at St. James's Palace and runs up to the road
against Albemarle Buildings. It was a spacious street, with
good houses, inhabited by gentry. In the eighteenth century,
famous clubs and gaming houses were located on St. James's
Street: White's Chocolate House, Boodle's, and Crockford's.

43.   (p. 111) *hackney-coach* a four-wheeled coach, drawn by two
horses and seated for six persons, kept for hire (*OED*).

44. (p. 114) *Catharine, on quitting the chamber, locked the door on the outside, taking with her the key* In Ann Radcliffe's *The Mysteries of Udolpho* (1794), the heroine, Emily St. Aubert experiences a similar fear when she finds that her door "had no bolts on the chamber side, though it had two on the other" (Oxford World's Classics, 235). Feminist critics have suggested that the Gothic house is a symbolic representation of a woman's body with its many unlit passageways. That the door can be opened or closed only from the outside suggests the loss of control and vulnerability of the female body (see Cynthia Griffin Wolff, "The Radcliffean Gothic Model: A Form for Feminine Sexuality" in *The Female Gothic*, ed. Juliann E. Fleenor, Montreal: Eden, 1983, pp. 207–223).

45. (p. 118) *Think not, by feeble restraints, to fetter the body when the mind is determined and free* In *Letters and Essays*, Hays writes: "bolts and bars may confine for a time the feeble body, but can never enchain the noble, the free-born mind" (Garland 23).

In *Enquiry Concerning Political Justice* William Godwin asserts that force or authority cannot control man, that "government is founded in opinion" (130). Hays is influenced by his beliefs that freedom is more a state of mind than a physical condition. Godwin: "Make men wise, and by that very operation you make them free. Civil liberty follows as a consequence of this; no usurped power can stand against the artillery of opinion" (Clarendon IV:i, 134).

46. (p. 118) *liberty, the common right of a human being* On independence or liberty, William Godwin makes the following distinction in *Enquiry Concerning Political Justice*: "Natural independence, a freedom from all constraint, ex-

cept that of reasons and inducements presented to the understanding, is of the utmost importance to the welfare and improvement of mind. Moral independence, on the contrary, is always injurious . . . because it is exercised clandestinely, and because we submit to its operation with impatience and aversion" (VIII:viii, 299).

47. (p. 122) *I felt guarded as by a talisman, encompassed in a magic circle, through which neither danger could assail nor sorrow pierce me* Hays has used the metaphor of the magic circle in other works to suggest the confinement of women by custom or patriarchal society (see note 39, for example). This should signal to the reader that the security she feels with William Pelham is a false or confining one.

48. (p. 129) *enthusiast* one who is full of 'enthusiasm' for a cause or principle, or who enters with enthusiasm into a pursuit . . . sometimes with unfavourable notions; a visionary, self-deluded person.

49. (p. 131) *a small Morocco case* Morocco leather was made from goatskins, tanned with sumac, and was originally produced in Morocco and other Barbary States. It was usually black or red.

50. (p. 148) *A sheriff's officer, who have, from courtesy, brought you to my own house* The sheriff was an officer to whom was entrusted in each county the execution of the laws. As Mary is unable to pay her creditors, she could be conducted to debtor's prison.

51. (p. 165) *a tour to the western islands* the Hebrides, or Western Islands of Scotland. The most famous tour of the western islands in the eighteenth century is the one made by

Samuel Johnson and James Boswell in the autumn of 1773. See Johnson's *A Journey to the Western Islands of Scotland* (1775) and Boswell's *The Journal of a Tour to the Hebrides with Samuel Johnson* (1785).

52.   (p. 167) *Gathering in the wind,/ Still shew'd my instant foes behind* From Edward Moore's Fable XV, "The Female Seducers":

But echo gathers in the wind,
And shows her instant foes behind.

Fables for the Female Sex, 3rd Ed. (London: T. Davies & J. Dodsley, 1766, p. 140). The passage occurs after the maiden has lost her chastity. She attempts to go back to the "land of virtue" and finds only hostility from her friends.

53.   (p. 168) *mephitic* a noxious vapour; having the character of a noxious or pestilential emanation, especially from the earth (*OED*).

Select Bibliography

Blain, Virginia, Isobel Grundy, & Patricia Clements, eds. *The Feminist Companion to Literature in English: Women Writers from the Middle Ages to the Present.* New Haven: Yale UP, 1990.

Butler, Marilyn. *Jane Austen and the War of Ideas.* Oxford: Clarendon, 1975; rprnt 1989.

Doody, Margaret Anne. "English Women Novelists and the French Revolution." *La femme en Angleterre et dans les colonies américaines aux XVIIe et XVIIIe siècles.* Paris: Actes du Colloque tenir à Paris, Université de Lille III, 1975: 176–198.

Hoagwood, Terence Allan. Introduction to *Victim of Prejudice.* By Mary Hays. Delmar, N.Y: Scholars' Facsimiles & Reprints, 1990.

Johnson, Claudia L. *Jane Austen: Women, Politics, and the Novel.* Chicago: U of Chicago P, 1988.

Kelly, Gary. *Women, Writing, and Revolution 1790–1827* Oxford: Clarendon, 1993.

Kelly, Gary. *English Fiction of the Romantic Period 1789–1830.* London: Longman Literature in English Series, 1989.

---. *The English Jacobin Novel 1780–1805.* Oxford: Clarendon, 1976.

Luria, Gina. "Mary Hays: A Critical Biography." Diss. New York University, 1972.

---. "Mary Hays's Letters & Manuscripts." *Signs: Journal of Women in Culture and Society.* 3.2 (Winter 1977):524–530.

Pollin, Burton R. "Mary Hays on Women's Rights in the *Monthly Magazine.*" *Etudes Anglaises.* 24.3 (1971):271-282.

Rogers, Katharine M. "The Contribution of Mary Hays." *Prose Studies* 10.2 (September 1987):131-142.

Spencer, Jane. *The Rise of the Woman Novelist: From Aphra Behn to Jane Austen.* Oxford: Blackwell, 1986.

Spender, Dale. *Mothers of the Novel: 100 Good Women Writers before Jane Austen.* New York: Pandora, 1986.

Todd, Janet, ed. *A Dictionary of British and American Women Writers 1660-1800.* Totowa, N.J.: Rowman & Littlefield, 1987.

Todd, Janet. *The Sign of Angellica: Women, Writing and Fiction, 1660-1800.* London: Virago, 1989.

Tompkins, J.M.S. *The Popular Novel in England 1770-1800.* London: Constable, 1932.

Ty, Eleanor. *Unsex'd Revolutionaries: Five Women Novelists of the 1790s.* Toronto: U of Toronto P, 1993.

Watson, Nicola J. *Revolution and the Form of the British Novel, 1790-1825: Intercepted Letters, Interrupted Seductions.* Oxford: Clarendon, 1994.

A Chronology of Mary Hays

1760   Born into large Dissenting family in Southwark, near London.

1777   Met and fell in love with John Eccles. Relationship disapproved by both families.

1778-80 Intimate correspondence with Eccles, her lover and "monitor."

1780   Engagement meets approval of the families.

        (August 23) Death of John Eccles from fever.

1782   Begins correspondence with rational Dissenter and opponent of the slave trade, Robert Robinson, about Deism and other theological subjects.

1786   "The Hermit: An Oriental Tale" published in the *Universal Magazine*.

1791   *Cursory Remarks on an Enquiry into the Expediencey and Propriety of Public or Social Worship: Inscribed to Gilbert Wakefield.*

1792   Read Mary Wollstonecraft's *A Vindication of the Rights of Woman*. Introduced to Wollstonecraft by George Dyer.

1793   *Letters and Essays, Moral and Miscellaneous.*

Wrote to William Godwin to borrow his copy of *Enquiry Concerning Political Justice*. Six year friendship with Godwin begins.

1796   (January) Invites William Godwin, Mary Wollstonecraft, and Thomas Holcroft to tea at her home.

Confesses to William Frend about her secret love for him.

(November) *Memoirs of Emma Courtney.*

1796-97   Contributor to the *Monthly Magazine*. Began to review novels for the *Analytical Review*.

1797   Published unsigned obituary of Mary Wollstonecraft in the September issue of the *Monthly Magazine*.

1798   *Appeal to the Men of Great Britain in Behalf of Women* published anonymously by Joseph Johnson.

1799   *The Victim of Prejudice.*

Close association with Romantic writers — Robert Southey, Samuel Taylor Coleridge, and Charles Lloyd.

1800   Second obituary of Wollstonecraft published in *Annual Necrology, 1797-1798*.

Friendship with Eliza Fenwick and Henry Crabb Robinson.

1803   *Female Biography; or, Memoirs of Illustrious and Celebrated Women, of All Ages and Countries.*

1804   *Harry Clinton; or a Tale of Youth.*

1806-08 Historical Dialogues for Young Persons.

1806   *The History of England, from the Earliest Records to the Peace of Amiens; in a Series of Letters to a Young Lady at School.* Written with Charlotte Smith.

1807   Co-authored "Life" of Charlotte Smith with Smith for Richard Phillips' *Public Characters of 1800-1801.*

1814   Stayed in Hot Wells, Clifton with Mrs. Pennington. Influenced by works of Hannah More and Maria Edgeworth.

1815   *The Brothers; or Consequences: A Story of What Happens Every Day; Addressed to that Most Useful Part of the Community, the Labouring Poor.*

1817   *Family Annals; or the Sisters.*

1821   *Memoirs of Queens Illustrious and Celebrated.*

1843   Died at eighty-three years old. Requested to be buried in Newington cemetery with the simple memorial "Mary Hays" engraved on the headstone.

Acknowledgements

Wilfrid Laurier University's generous book preparation grant enabled me to complete this edition and to do research at the Bancroft Library, University of California, Berkeley, at the Huntington Library, and at the Department of Special Collections, University of California, Los Angeles. I would like to thank Gary Kelly for sharing his expertise in revolutionary writers of the period with me, and for allowing me to read his chapters on Hays from *Women, Writing, and Revolution, 1790–1827* in manuscript form. I am grateful for the intellectual and moral support of my colleagues in the English Department at Laurier, in particular, Viviana Comensoli, Gary Boire, Jane Campbell, Anne Russell, and Lynn Shakinovsky. I have benefited from the friendship, words of wisdom, and encouragement of Susan Bennett and Nancy Copeland. Finally, thanks to Jason and David Hunter for their love and patience.